Don't Pull Your Sister's Hair

DON'T PULL
—YOUR—
SISTER'S
HAIR

**And Other Life Lessons
Growing Up Neurodiverse**

SAM FLOOD JR.

NEW YORK

LONDON • NASHVILLE • MELBOURNE • VANCOUVER

DON'T PULL YOUR SISTER'S HAIR

And Other Life Lessons Growing Up Neurodiverse

Published in New York, New York, by Morgan James Publishing. Morgan James is a trademark of Morgan James, LLC. www.MorganJamesPublishing.com

Proudly distributed by Publishers Group West®

A **FREE** ebook edition is available for you
or a friend with the purchase of this print book.

CLEARLY SIGN YOUR NAME ABOVE

Instructions to claim your free ebook edition:
1. Visit MorganJamesBOGO.com
2. Sign your name CLEARLY in the space above
3. Complete the form and submit a photo
   of this entire page
4. You or your friend can download the ebook
   to your preferred device

ISBN 9781636985565 paperback
ISBN 9781636985572 ebook
Library of Congress Control Number:
2024943494

Cover Design by:
Christopher Kirk
www.GFSstudio.com

Interior Design by:
Chris Treccani
www.3dogcreative.net

Morgan James is a proud partner of Habitat for Humanity Peninsula
and Greater Williamsburg. Partners in building since 2006.

Get involved today! Visit: www.morgan-james-publishing.com/giving-back

Contents

Dedication

To my mom who always believed in me, always fought for me and gave me the opportunity to live this amazing life.

Foreword

My guess is God looks at success very differently than most of us. Each success must be measured independently against a backdrop of challenges. Like many, I have always been drawn to stories of people who have had to overcome obstacles and burdens. That is why I have always been so intrigued with the story of my friend Samuel Elliot Flood Jr.

Sammy never spoke until he was five years old. Luckily, Sammy had his four-year-old sister Eliza and her beautiful blonde locks of hair to help him. When Sammy needed, or wanted something, he would pull his older sister's hair. Eliza would then tell her mother Jane what Sammy wanted. No kidding. But, by age five Sammy no longer needed hair translations, he was communicating on his own.

Unfortunately, the world can be very unkind to those whose successes are unique. Who could blame parents for wanting to protect their child from such circumstances? But that was not the path chosen for Sammy by parents Sam and Jane Flood. They chose the deep end of the pool, all the while watching with life preserver in hand. How difficult it must have been to watch Sammy struggle with otherwise normal daily interactions. They watched him fail but grow many times. They ignored the pessimism of doctors and introduced greater, and greater challenges to Sammy.

Many parents would have felt embarrassed for their child and for themselves. But the greater goal was always in focus, preparing Sammy for the world he would face alone. The successes are heart-warming, but the pain is palpable.

When I learned that Sammy was writing fiction, my question was simple, why fiction? How interesting would it be to tap into Sammy's mind, and listen to the stories from his perspective. What would we all learn that only he could teach us. Apparently, I wasn't the only one who wanted to read this story.

I hope you enjoy *Don't Pull Your Sister's Hair*. When I was shown the title all I could think was, thank God he did.

—**Cris Collinsworth**, 17-time Emmy Award Winning analyst for NBC Sunday Night Football

Preface:
Who Am I?

Hey there! My name is Samuel Elliot Flood, Jr., but you can call me Sam for short. Right now, I live in a penthouse in Ridgewood, New Jersey. Okay, it's not really a penthouse. Actually, it's the third floor of my family's house on the outskirts of New York City, but it's fun to dream.

When I first moved to this house, I was an out of control two-year-old boy.

My sister Eliza was four and had the thickest, curliest blonde hair imaginable. Apparently, at age two, I decided the best way to communicate was by pulling her hair. I didn't speak until I was five, so as a nonverbal two-year-old child, I couldn't ask for help.

Eliza would scream as I pulled her hair, and my parents would dash to the rescue. She would say, "Sammy wants orange juice," or "He needs a snack" or "Sammy wants to watch TV." Somehow, she could translate my hair pulling and figure out what I wanted.

Fortunately, I eventually learned how to talk, and my sister still has a nice head of curly blonde hair. Mine is the story of how I went from being a boy unable to communicate to a man who wants to write books and tell stories for a living.

Obviously, my inability to speak concerned my parents, Sam and Jane, and they took me to doctors to figure out what was wrong.

One specialist said I would never graduate from high school, let alone go to college. Well, I managed to graduate from high school and earned a BA from Mitchell College in New London, Connecticut.

I have asked my parents to add their insights to events I describe and to explain what they experienced as I evolved from a "wild child" to the man I am today. Some of their stories were news to me, including the specialist telling my parents that my educational opportunities would be limited. I'm glad they didn't listen to that doctor.

This is the story of what is possible.

— Chapter 1: —

The Hair-Pulling, Wild-Child Toddler Years

(1995–1999)

I don't remember much about my years as a baby or a toddler. Does anyone really remember their first few years on earth? Most early childhoods become glamorized by parents, grandparents, and older siblings. Those glowing stories of the first years of someone's life are usually enchanting.

Not so much in my case.

I was supposed to be born on December 18, 1993, but for some reason, I decided I wanted to wait until 1994. I finally arrived on New Year's Day, two weeks late. Mom said that during those two weeks, she was so pregnant that she could barely fit behind the steering wheel of the car. My mother struggled to chase down my sister Eliza, who is two years older than me, as she bounced around our house in Ridgewood, New Jersey.

When my parents brought me home from the hospital, Eliza ran toward me and hugged me so hard that Mom had to tell her to be gentle with me. So Eliza pulled back and petted me like a dog.

I was so chubby when I was born that my parents called me "Buddha Baby." I was a mellow and calm baby, but that would soon change.

Looking back on all that Sammy has accomplished and at the tremendous person he has become, it is sometimes hard to remember what it was like when he was a baby. Parenthood is the most exciting, scary, and rewarding thing you can do in your life. Having my second child, I assumed I had the whole pregnancy, delivery, and newborn thing down pat.

If you think you have parenthood figured out, you do not! After some minor health issues during pregnancy, our beautiful, happy, and healthy baby girl, Eliza, was born. I went back to work when she was three months old, and besides being tired by the end of the work week, I really thought parenting was relatively easy.

From the outset, Sammy seemed to have his own idea for how life should be, from arriving two weeks late, to walking (and running) at ten months, to not talking at all until the age of four.

Of course, I am biased, but Sammy was by far the most beautiful baby boy ever. He was a very big but calm and happy baby. In hindsight, he may have been too calm. He rarely cried, and he slept through the night at about five weeks old. Sammy was always extremely alert; his eyes followed us around the room. He was often restless and seemed happiest when he was moving, whether in the stroller, car seat, or someone's arms.

When he began to walk and move around on his own, it became apparent that Sammy was a very different child than Eliza. She could speak at a relatively young age, and she loved to talk and tell what she did and didn't want. Sammy did not speak at all, and from the moment he was able, he was on the move.

—Mom, Jane Flood

I was born two weeks late, and I always felt I was late to the major events in my life. I was five years old when I started talking, nineteen when I graduated from high school, and twenty-four when I graduated from college. But I started walking when I was ten months old. So, I was on my feet and active early. I took my first steps during my grandmother's fifty-ninth birthday party, and those steps turned into full sprints in just a few days. I ran around the house, and my parents were amazed how agile and quick I was. They felt proud that I could walk so early in life. While the walking came quickly, the talking was another matter and one main reason for this book.

Ten toes, ten fingers, and a loud cry as Sammy finally joined us two weeks late. The first few months were chaos as we adjusted from just chatty Eliza to two kids and plenty of diapers. Boys are different from girls, but we slowly started to realize that silent Sammy was not developing the same way Eliza ticked off the milestones. Sure, Sammy was an early walker and a terror on two feet, but he never said a word and was happy to chill by himself.

—Dad, Sam Flood

Wild Animal Child

My parents described me as "out of control," a "pain in the neck," a "punk" or a "little monster." Around age one, I started pulling my sister's hair to get my parents' attention. Eliza's hair became my way of communicating with the family.

My sister later said she was traumatized by the hair pulling and loved to tell dramatic stories of my antics. Eliza was a bit of a theater geek and acted in many of the plays in high school and college, so she certainly knew drama.

That said, I was very lucky she handled the hair pulling period so well. For some crazy reason, she always knew why I was upset and would tell my parents what would calm the situation.

Mom would pry each of my fingers out of the death lock on Eliza's blond hair. A few strands would be stuck in my clenched fists. My family was astounded at how Eliza knew what had set me into a hair pulling tirade and how to solve it. Often, it was a simple, "He is hungry," or "He lost his toy," or "Turn on Barney the Purple Dinosaur."

> Not only could Sammy not speak, but he also seemed to not understand or acknowledge anyone that spoke to him. Sammy went and did whatever he wanted. Whenever we tried to control Sammy, he acted out, squirming, running away. Eliza has the most beautiful blonde curly hair, and Sammy's preferred method of getting our attention was to pull her hair. This behavior got worse the more frustrated he became. We would have to pry his fingers loose from her hair. The older he got, the more chaotic our household became.
>
> —Mom, Jane Flood

How My Life Changed

Hair pulling was not the only way I expressed myself. Mom said I used to get a goofy grin on my face when I decided I would poop in the bathtub. Mom would have to drain the tub, clean it with Clorox, and throw me back in.

I also liked to write on the walls, tear off wallpaper, and generally create constant chaos.

One morning when I was three years old, my parents heard a knock on the door and came downstairs to find a neighbor holding my hand, asking my mom and dad if they were missing someone. Apparently, this neighbor had a piano, and that morning, I got up early, walked down the street, entered their house through the front door, sat down, and started pounding on the piano. Since I couldn't talk, there was no way for us to communicate; they helplessly pleaded with me to go back home until they had to walk me there.

Also when I was three, my parents couldn't find me, and they scoured the neighborhood screaming my name. Earlier that day, my parents had promised Eliza and me an ice cream trip in downtown Ridgewood. Apparently I was sick of waiting, so I decided to go alone. They found me a block from Häagen Dazs, wandering around with a cone in my hand. Häagen Dazs was a ten-minute walk from my house, all the way to downtown, near the train station. I guess I knew it wasn't very far, and I wanted my ice cream.

I was always curious about the items of my surrounding area and wanted to know how they work and what makes them tick.

Early Learning

My parents put me in a preschool program, but after one day, we never returned. They decided that being in the program was not a good idea, mainly because I was making a ruckus in the classroom. By that time, my parents were taking me to specialists to figure out why I couldn't talk and why I was so uncontrollable. I was also getting a series of ear infections, and my parents thought that might be affecting my hearing. First was the hospital in Hackensack, where doctors gave me a series of tests and studied my behavior.

They concluded that I had little chance of success. They told my parents that I needed to be placed in special classes and would probably never graduate from high school, let alone college. One doctor said that my parents should go home, cry, and accept that it was going to be a difficult time raising a child with these issues.

I wish I could hand those doctors a copy of this book and my bachelors degree.

It's safe to say that growing up with Sammy was never boring or predictable. He was the perfect constant playmate and best friend to a little girl desperate for a forever friend who wouldn't disappear when the story ended. There are very few memories I have from our childhood, but there are flashes of "Sammy, no!" and Mom screaming. Thankfully, I don't remember the pain of the hair pulling, but I know the impact it had on our family.

His violent actions became the catalyst for change in our family dynamic. Almost overnight, it went from being Eliza and Sammy to Sammy and Eliza. The subtle shift wasn't apparent at first. We were both so young that one child getting more attention wasn't obvious. But as we got older, it became more obvious and somehow easier to ignore. Mom, Dad, and Sammy created a special bond that I often observed from the outside. I wasn't in the room learning with our parents about how to help Sammy; I was in the waiting room with a book, desperate for it all to be over so I could go home and play.

—Sister, Eliza

I've learned there is always a silver lining. It was clear that this was a total lifestyle change for us all and we were in for a long haul. Despite the bleak situation, we had options and a path out of the family chaos.

It would definitely not be easy or quick, but we could see results. As a parent, you have to accept the challenge and work to better your child's situation. The severity of Sammy's behavior turned out to be the silver lining. Eliza could definitely not wait for Sammy to "outgrow" his hair pulling; we had to act immediately. Drastic measures were warranted, and we plunged wholeheartedly into this therapy.

—Mom, Jane Flood

My parents never gave up on me, so they decided to get a second opinion. Through my grandfather, Dick Flood, they were able to contact a famous doctor in New York City. I call him Dr. Helper because he helped change my life.

When my parents drove me into New York City for the first time, I was amazed at the enormous size of the buildings and how loud and crowded the city was. I had spent most of my toddler years in quiet Ridgewood, but in New York City, I felt like I was part of a bigger world. When I first met Dr. Helper, I was shy because not only was he a new person I had just met, but also he towered over me. Dr. Helper said that I was diagnosed with ADHD, attention-deficit hyperactivity disorder, and language processing issues, a disability which might lead me to misinterpret what other people are saying. He believed that my mind was in complete chaos, and I needed order and balance. So, Dr. Helper suggested that my mom and dad visit a behavioral and language therapist. I like to call her Dr. Lifechanger because she changed my life.

We are fortunate to come from a family of educators. My father, Dick Flood, better known as Floodo, was the headmaster at Salisbury School from 1988–2003. The thousands of students Floodo impacted through the years gave him a Rolodex of families who faced challenges with their children. There were plenty of stories of kids who overcame similar hurdles to graduate from college and continue on to have amazing careers. One parent told Floodo about their son who didn't speak until he was four or five and faced language processing challenges. The family had worked with a doctor in New York, whom Sammy now calls Dr. Helper.

We went to our first meeting with Dr. Helper prepared for more tough news about Sammy's prospects. The three of us entered the small, narrow office where we met Dr. Helper. One wall was packed with books, and on the lower shelves were boxes of toys. Sammy started spinning around the room and grabbing toys and plastic soldiers out of the boxes. He was making a mess. The doctor calmly asked us about Sammy and his development.

Down on the rug, Sammy was setting up a battle scene between two sets of plastic figures. It looked like chaos, but Sammy was creating some sort of order out of the men.

Dr. Helper said, "Your son does not look at the toys as chunks of plastic but rather as soldiers and men." He said that was great news and meant Sammy understood the world around him. The challenge was figuring out how to get him to join our world and create order. The doctor didn't want to label Sammy beyond saying he had a language processing disorder and clear attention issues. The first step was getting the wild child under control. Everyone needs and wants control in their lives, and this meant another doctor and a new challenge.

—Dad, Sam Flood

When we first arrived at her house, Dr. Lifechanger explained to my parents that I needed to be brought under control like a wild animal. Dr. Lifechanger believed that I had to learn how to listen, sit still, and follow directions. That was impossible for me.

She told me to sit on a chair and be still. There was no way I could do it. So she sat on the floor and wrapped her arms and legs around me so I could not move for the next thirty minutes.

I struggled and tried to break away from her, but after thirty minutes, I calmed down, and she released me.

In simple terms, Dr. Lifechanger's program is like breaking a horse. The concept was that once Sammy was under control, he would see that the world was not so overwhelming. This sounds easy, but in reality, making it happen was at times excruciating. Dr. Lifechanger demonstrated that we needed to give Sammy a simple command, "sit" or "do this" in as few words as possible. If he did not do what we asked, we would have to immobilize him in a bear hug until he was compliant. Dr. Lifechanger demonstrated for us and said it could take as long as thirty to forty minutes to achieve compliance. Watching Sammy kick, scream, and cry for those almost forty minutes was one of the hardest things I have ever experienced. The phrase "crawling out of one's skin" comes to mind. Once Sammy stopped fighting, he became very calm and sat next to Dr. Lifechanger and wanted to hold her hand. He then very calmly did what was asked of him. As drastic as it seemed, it worked, and we were on board.

Dr. Lifechanger then explained that we would have to do this at home with Sammy, but most importantly, we needed to be fully committed. There was no way to partially do this therapy, which is why about 65 to 70 percent of the parents that came to Dr. Lifechanger chose not to pursue it. We were to start with three of Sammy's behaviors that needed to be corrected immediately and report back in two weeks. The first three behaviors were easy: do not pull Eliza's hair, keep his socks and shoes on, and sit at the table while he was eating. Most importantly, we needed to ignore behaviors if we were not in the position to subdue Sammy in the bear hug. There could be no mixed signals.

The first two weeks were difficult, but the results were undeniable. Sammy immediately became more compliant, especially with the hair pulling. Eliza was less traumatized, and our house was more peaceful.

—Mom, Jane Flood

When my parents practiced Dr. Lifechanger's exercise, they would stay in the room holding me for thirty minutes until I calmed down. Her theory was that everyone wanted order in their life, and I had only chaos. I wouldn't wear my shoes, wouldn't sit quietly at the dinner table, wouldn't sit still in the grocery cart, and wouldn't settle in my car seat. One time, when my mom took me to a Stop & Shop, I had a meltdown because my mom wouldn't let me get the candy I wanted. I was also disturbed by all the noise in the store. Because I couldn't talk, I couldn't tell her what I wanted. She ended up having to drag me out of the store after I pulled all of the candy off the shelf into the aisle.

Dr. Lifechanger worked out of her house in New Jersey. The three of us arrived and were greeted by this tiny woman with a German accent and powerful presence. She described her process and the outcome. As Sammy wandered about the room, grabbing blocks and toys, Dr. Lifechanger commanded him to sit still. The little dude wanted no part of sitting still or paying attention. This is when Dr. Lifechanger got down on the floor and sat with her arms and legs wrapped around Sammy so he could not move. She calmly told us that many parents watch their child struggle to escape her grasp, and they leave after ten minutes, but if we could handle thirty minutes of the clawing, screaming, crying, and screeching, Sammy would become compliant.

Jane and I looked at each other not knowing what was about to happen, but we trusted the process. We would try anything to help stop the chaos in Sammy's world.

The next thirty minutes were much worse than we expected. Sammy was terrified; his tears, screams, and attempts to bite the doctor were awful. Through the chaos, Dr. Lifechanger calmly talked to us as though nothing was out of the ordinary. She navigated the biting attempts, the headbutts, and the fists of fury.

We were desperate to help Sammy, but was it too mean? Was it even helpful, breaking the spirit and creating such emotional pain for a three year old? We were torn, but the doctor said: "Imagine what happens if he is fully grown and out of control like this. What happens then?"

At the thirty-minute mark, as if by magic, Sammy went limp. The crying turned into a tiny whimper, and Dr. Lifechanger started controlling him. He was compliant, and so began the process of joining the world: step one of learning language and communication.

This is where Jane made one of her many sacrifices to break the chain of chaos. She completely shut down her life outside the house to bring Sammy under control. Jane became Dr. Lifechanger at home and had to manage Sammy with the same bear-hug technique.

—Dad, Sam Flood

The first few weeks under Dr. Lifechanger's program were not easy. The results were small changes that came from a tremendous amount of effort and patience. Even little changes in Sammy's behavior were a victory. We were moving in the right direction, but it was slow and exhausting for all.

Several weeks into the process I thought it was possible to venture out and test Sammy's behavior. Sam had been traveling with work and I really needed to grocery shop. After dropping Eliza off at preschool, we went to the food store. Our cart was full, and we were almost done when Sammy started throwing things out of the cart and pulling things off the shelves. When I told him NO in my firm but quiet voice (as instructed), Sammy had a complete screaming meltdown. As per the program, I had to remove him from the store immediately. I wheeled my full cart and screaming child to the manager's desk. I apologized for leaving the full cart and went home.

It was a momentary set back, but we still needed food. Too embarrassed to go back to the same grocery store, Sammy and I calmed down and went to a different store. This time it was a quick trip for a few basics and then back to preschool to pick up Eliza. Sammy and I were both so happy to see adorable, happy Eliza and all seemed okay again. Dinner would be fast food drive thru. We would try another day - the program had to succeed.

-Mom, Jane Flood

Dr. Lifechanger said I couldn't talk because my mind was jumbled with images in my head. She believed that I had an excellent visual memory for pictures and images but not for words. She believed that if I visualized words more, I might remember the right ones to say.

When I was calm and sat still, my mom and dad used wooden blocks to help me create sentences. For hours, I'd try to memorize the order of red, blue, green, and yellow blocks as my parents mixed up the arrangement. It was frustrating at first but became easier as I rearranged each word block to make sentences.

Getting My Life on the Right Track

At age five, I was finally able to talk. My first word was *Mom*. My parents hired a speech therapist named Kathy Gallagher to help me speak correctly. She was a tall, blonde, pretty lady who had a very big personality. She was talkative and outgoing, and she would not let me daydream in my own little world. Kathy insisted I talk with her instead.

Because of my work with Dr. Lifechanger and Kathy, when I turned five years old, I was able to start preschool at the Glen School in Ridgewood, where there were programs for kids like me who needed extra help and attention. I was terrified during my first few days of preschool. I cried and tried to hang on to my mom when she was about to leave, so she had to sneak away from me when I was distracted.

When I was attending the Glen School at the age of four, I fell playing at the playground, hurting my shoulder in the process. I was sobbing because my shoulder was broken, or so I believed. And since I couldn't talk back then, the teachers didn't know what to do with me. They tried to call my mom, but she was unavailable, and so they turned to my emergency contacts, Uncle Terry and Aunt Kathryn. Terry responded and drove to pick me up. When I saw Terry's car parked near the school, I held my arms up and ran to hug him when he got out of the car. The teachers told my mom that I was happy when I saw Terry. The important thing is that Terry was my go-to guy, even when I didn't speak back then.

Having a child who learns differently teaches you to manage expectations, most importantly your own expectations as a parent. The early behavioral therapy I did with Sammy was exhausting and often frustrating. Progress was evident, but the more we got into it, the more it was apparent that there was no magic bullet and we were in for the long haul. I was feeling better about Sammy's behavior being more under control, but school seemed like a real challenge. Once we had subdued Sammy's more egregious behaviors, Dr. Lifechanger suggested that we try to enroll him in a local preschool. Our first attempt was not remotely successful. Sammy screamed and refused to let me leave the room. It was suggested that we try our town's supported preschool program. I was hesitant to put Sammy (or myself) through that trauma again. The director of our town's special education program came to our house to evaluate Sammy. She observed him at play in the security of his own home and felt that he would do well in the program. If Sammy were comfortable enough to stay in a classroom and not have a meltdown, then that would be great progress.

—Mom, Jane Flood

My teacher, Ms. Vandersnow, was kind and patient. When I attended preschool, I was still wearing diapers. But after seeing my peers line up to go to the bathroom, I felt a little left out, which led me to use the toilet for the first time. My parents were amazed because they had tried for ages to get me to go to the bathroom on my own. Ms. Vandersnow said that I wanted to be like the other kids. Although I was scared at first, I enjoyed being in school because I was with people my own age, and it was always very important to be like the other kids.

Once I was physically under control and learned how to sit still, we saw Dr. Lifechanger less frequently. From then on, we kept visiting Dr. Helper. I still see him three or four times a year.

When I got older, my parents told me all kinds of funny stories, and my sister Eliza called me a name for pulling her hair. I still cannot entirely believe that I was an uncontrollable monster when I was a toddler. But thanks to the right people, mainly Dr. Lifechanger and Dr. Helper, I feel I am now in control of my emotions. Every time my family talks about our childhood, either Eliza or my parents remind me that I yanked my sister's hair or how my hands were filled with her hair. But isn't that the role of a little brother, to be a pain to their older sister?

Imagine being told by a doctor that your child would never graduate high school let alone go to college. Imagine being told your two-year-old son might need to be institutionalized one day. You can accept the diagnosis and go home and cry, as the doctor at Hackensack Medical Center suggested, or you can get to work. There are no guarantees in life or with children who develop differently, and we had no understanding of the crooked road that lay ahead. Instead of going home and crying, we got to work learning everything we could about language processing and speech. We read, researched, and looked for professional connections that could help navigate the learning and developmental disability maze.

One doctor told us that Sammy was probably autistic and would probably never learn to communicate. We were told to lower our expectations and think about an institutional placement for him. As the shock of this gut punch slowly wore off, the anger started to grow. That doctor had spent about fifteen to twenty minutes trying to talk to Sammy to reach the diagnosis. Sam and I both felt that this could not and would not be the final answer. Obviously, we needed more testing, more research, more information.

Fortunately, Sammy's grandfather, Floodo, had spent his whole life in education. He was immediately able to connect us with an expert in child development that he had met in his capacity as the headmaster of a boarding school. We were at a very low point when we first met Dr. Helper. Still reeling from the original diagnosis, we took Sammy to see Dr. Helper so that we could strategize on the best care for him.

Dr. Helper observed Sammy and had a complete neuropsychological examination done. He told us that Sammy was not the classic definition of autistic but that he had ADHD and significant language processing issues. He recommended that we immediately start therapy with Dr. Lifesaver, who was a leader in behavioral and language therapy.

Both doctors felt that Sammy craved order in his world. He acted out because he lived in a constant state of sensory overload. He could not filter out outside stimulus. The chaos he found in the everyday created tremendous anxiety, and consequently, he acted out. We asked if it was possible that Sammy may grow out of this stage, as the behavioral therapy seemed extreme. Dr. Helper calmly asked if our daughter could afford to wait. Of course, that put everything in perspective.

There will never be a day that I wish Sammy was different, but every day, I wish things had been easier for him. That he was able to convey his feelings earlier without aggression, that he never had to see Dr. Helper, that Mom and Dad never had to worry that he wouldn't have the same opportunities as other children. Sammy is an inspiration, a gentle giant (though you would have never guessed it from our early days), and the most incredible brother. Everything has worked out the way it was supposed to. We are incredibly lucky to have the wonderful doctors, psychiatrists, supportive parents, grandparents, aunts, uncles, and cousins who all embraced Sammy with open hearts.

—**Dad, Sam Flood**

LIFE LESSONS

Learn to control your temper.

Be thankful to those who helped you.

Always value family above all else.

Find order in chaos.

Explore your world.

Chapter 2:
Childhood From Six to Eleven
(2000–2005)

The memories become more vivid from these years—fond memories of elementary school and becoming fascinated by TV shows, video games, and comics. I also spent a great deal of time with my family, of course.

Saturday Morning Cartoons

When I was around five or six years old, playgrounds became my escape and showed me what adventures life had to offer. I didn't know much about the positives and negatives of the world because I was young, but I thought that life was just a fairytale with happy endings where boy meets girl or girl meets boy and they automatically marry without getting to know each other. These were the kinds of worlds kids used to see in Disney movies or animated movies. That is how I viewed life when I was little, just a Disney or animated film where I felt I was going on an adventure in the movie.

I did not understand the realities of the world back then.

I remember watching Saturday morning shows like *Power Rangers* (Mainly *In Space* and *Lost Galaxy*), *Transformers Beast Wars*, *Batman the Animated Series*, and *Spider-Man the Animated Series*, and I was amazed at how those shows took me to adventures in outer space or remote places on earth. Those shows are nostalgic to me; they were something I could wake up to every Saturday morning, shows with action and excitement.

School Life

After preschool at the Glen School, I spent kindergarten and first grade in the supported classroom for kids with learning disabilities at Somerville School. I didn't know that I was different from the rest of my peers back then, and when I was sent to this "special" class because of my ADHD, I felt like I wasn't learning very much. It seemed like we were just watching movies and listening to stories.

I was still struggling with how I communicated. Sometimes I said sentences that were incomplete, and these gaps concerned my parents. It was also difficult for me to pronounce certain words correctly. So, they signed me up with a communication specialist named Janet Krebs.

She and I saw each other after school, and we took part in speech activities as a way of helping me talk correctly. We mostly played computer games with levels based on completing sentences correctly. She also cut out pictures from magazines to help me figure out what a story was about and how to explain it properly. We would use toys to play out conversations that would help me communicate better.

There were other kids in Janet Krebs' program who were younger than me, and I felt like the black sheep, the outsider.

I'm not sure you are supposed to cry while reading your son's story about his elementary school years. A flood of memories hit me as I read Sammy's recollection of those years. It also made me think about how I treated people who learned, acted, or developed differently from the perceived norm.

Rather than writing about my recollections of these Sammy years, I'm going off script and looking at my own behavior when I was young. I wish I could turn back the clock and say sorry for not being more accepting of the kids who were different from my buddies. I wish I learned from those kids rather than disrespecting the challenges they faced. I wish I had been more patient with the Sammys of my youth and engaging instead of dismissing them. Sammy has taught me more about being a kind and compassionate human being than anyone else in my life. He is a remarkable man who overcame tremendous challenges to become my hero.

Sammy has taught me patience and compassion. His development might have taken longer and involved some complicated moments, but he never quit on himself or his opportunity to be great. He is great, and incredibly kind and caring about others. Unlike Sammy, I learned those lessons later in life because of him. When Sammy was born, I wanted a son to share hockey, baseball, and football with, but in reality, I won the lottery with a son who had so much more to offer. He taught me how to be a better and more patient man who accepts people for who they are and who they want to become. Sure, we would shoot hoops or play catch, but I realized Sammy did these things to make me happy. He was unselfish and clearly a bit uncomfortable saying, "No, Dad, I don't want to throw the ball back and forth with you." Eventually I understood what he wanted and how we could share moments and memories. We now share golf and walks around a golf course where we can talk or not talk. We share an experience and, most importantly, time.

—Dad, Sam Flood

I didn't want to be in the self-contained classroom at Somerville. I wanted to be at the Orchard School, which was our neighborhood school and where Eliza was in second grade. It was an all-day kindergarten for me in the Somerville program. I spent the morning in the contained classroom where we went over the basic skills of reading, spelling, and math. We had lunch at school and got to play outside during recess. I loved recess because, of course, I loved running around outside, but I also felt I was part of the whole school.

In the afternoon I went to a "regular" kindergarten with my other classmates. The morning class prepared me to do well in the afternoon class, where there were a lot more children. Since I wanted to be just like the other kids in the afternoon, I stayed focused on the morning work.

Small gestures and casual words can be inadvertently cruel or incredibly kind. The preschool program continued into the town's self-contained classroom. Sammy spent kindergarten and first grade in this program, which was in a different elementary school than ours. The program was excellent and expanded on the premise of the preschool program.

Two instances stand out in my mind from Sammy's time at that school. The first showed that even people who probably mean well can be very hurtful. Early in Sammy's time in kindergarten, a woman I knew from town saw me at after-school pick-up and asked if I had moved across town. When I explained that Sammy was in the self-contained program, she said she was happy he was doing well. When he ran over to us, she said: "What is wrong with him? He looks so normal." I know I am and will always be sensitive about Sammy. I do not think that woman realized how hurtful her words were. I am sure she meant well, but when you have struggled with your child's issues and come so far, it is hard to hear something that seems so negative.

The second instance showed how much simple acts of kindness can mean to others. In first grade, the regular class was doing a unit on poetry, and each student had to find a partner and recite a poem together for all the parents. Sammy seemed excited about the project, but I was nervous about his ability to speak in front of the class and parents. When his teacher asked to speak to me about the poetry project, I sensed a problem, and my heart sank a little. She explained the project and explained that there were many tears shed over finding partners. I immediately assumed that no one wanted to be Sammy's partner for the reading because of his difficulty with speech. The teacher explained that the tears were not Sammy's but were from three girls in the class. Apparently, three different girls asked Sammy to be their partner, and he said yes to all three. Fortunately, a compromise was reached, and Sammy was able to read parts of poems with all three girls. I am still so grateful for the kindness of those young girls to reach out to include the boy in the class who struggled with that type of assignment. It made me think of my own experiences in grade school.

There was a boy who was always getting in trouble and running away from school. We would laugh as the teachers chased him around the playground to try to get him back to class. He was considered the bad kid. Looking back, I wish I didn't laugh and was more understanding. The boy clearly had behavioral and attention issues that were most likely undiagnosed and unaddressed. Sitting at his desk all day was probably incredibly difficult for him.

—**Mom, Jane Flood**

First grade at Somerville was similar. I started the morning in the self-contained classroom before spending the afternoon in the regular first grade. I very much wanted to be like the other kids, so I would push the teachers to let me spend more time in the regular classroom. By the second month of school, my teachers decided I was ready to spend all day in the regular classroom.

I made enough progress that I was able to attend my neighborhood school, Orchard Elementary School, in second grade, and it was there I felt I began to learn. The assistant teacher was Mrs. X, who did most of my homework for me until she told my parents I should be doing my own homework, which I did after my dad criticized me.

When I was at school, I always felt different from my peers because of my learning disabilities of language processing and ADHD. I never fit in because I was mostly with my assistant teacher, away from my classmates. I had a chat with my dad a few months ago about my time at the Orchard School, and he said that I was different from my peers because of my learning disabilities. I didn't make a lot of friends at the school, he said, because I couldn't talk properly.

But my life at Somerville was not all that bad. A funny and inspiring moment happened during Spanish class in second grade. We took a test on translating English words into Spanish, and I was able to complete it on time. The Spanish teacher was shocked that I was able to answer all of the questions correctly. Because of my learning disabilities, she didn't believe I was able to do work at that level. She thought I cheated and gave me a bad score on the test.

I don't cheat. And my mom and I had studied together for the Spanish test, so she knew I was smart enough to get all the answers right. My mom was riled up and met with the Spanish teacher to make it clear I was smart and should not be treated like the class idiot. Eventually, my Spanish teacher gave me the good grade I should have earned after acing the test. The lesson here is that people should never doubt a person based on their learning disabilities. There might be more to that person than one might think.

Speech Therapy

Once I got into the Orchard School for the second grade, I was in a mainstream class and no longer in a self-contained classroom. I still had to go to speech therapy class to continue to speak properly. Every day, I had to report to speech class where my teacher, Ms. Michelle, had me learn how to speak properly by repeating what she said.

I always felt back then that I was wasting my time going to speech class when I could be learning so much with kids my age. It felt like I didn't belong in my main class, and I was different from the rest of my peers. My parents thought that because I couldn't talk properly, I had to go to speech class during school. I was furious that the other kids saw as I had to walk out of that classroom and into speech class, making me feel like I was the odd one and they were the normal ones. Back then, all I ever wanted was to fit in and be like everybody else—pulling pranks, tossing a ball back and forth, trying to pay attention to what the teacher was saying, taking part in a conversation at lunch, and watching TV after school during a weekday. But society seemed to believe I was different from everybody else because I couldn't talk right, stared off into space, and misinterpreted what other people were saying.

During fourth grade, my speech improved, and in the classroom, I felt I was becoming a more-active participant. I still had to be pulled out for speech therapy, which I did not like because it made me feel different and separate from my class. Ms. Michelle was supposed to come get me while the rest of the class was transitioning between lessons. One day, the timing did not work out, and

Ms. Michelle pulled me out in the middle of a lesson. I was really upset, so I yelled at her. I said, "I CAN'T STAND LIKE THAT!" in the accent of Dexter from *Dexter's Laboratory*, which was one of my favorite shows at the time. Dexter had a funny accent, and I realized I could mimic accents really well. My speech was really coming along, I thought. Unfortunately, my parents were not happy with my loud outburst and disrespect to the teacher.

They were also unimpressed with my ability to mimic Dexter's accent. I was never allowed to watch *Dexter's Laboratory* again. Fortunately, as I got older, I learned there were other great shows that are funny and fun to mimic. My friends and family love it now when I mimic these shows—when I joke around, of course. *Family Guy* voices are some of my favorites: Peter, Stewie, Lois, Quagmire, Joe, and Cleveland.

Learning Taekwondo

I was still working with Dr. Lifesaver, who suggested I take after-school taekwondo classes so I could learn more control and discipline. We found an amazing Korean man named Master Cha whose dojo was right down the street from our house. At the beginning, Master Cha gave me private lessons as he calmly taught me how to hold poses and execute taekwondo moves. Since I struggled in the loud group setting, it was very helpful to work in the controlled environment. Eventually I was allowed to join the group of fifteen boys and girls for the first ten minutes of a class. All the other children had belts of various colors. The order of our colored belts was first white, then yellow, green, red, blue, then brown, red-and-black, then black. The final belts are black. Mine was a simple white belt signifying that I was new to the sport and yet to attain any of the skills required to upgrade the belt.

At first, I was just goofing around the dojo, running around and playing with wooden sticks used as swords for practice. But Master Cha scolded me and said I needed to be focused during class. As punishment for lacking discipline, he had me do one hundred push-ups while the rest of the class watched. The first week was me doing push-ups whenever I messed up in class. I learned I had the control and discipline required to do all those solitary push-ups. I spent the next few years improving my skills, following instructions from Master Cha, and trying to keep up with the rest of my peers. I earned a yellow belt as a promotion for all of the time and focus I put into taekwondo class.

We usually had a belt test on Saturday mornings, when the students presented to the grand masters of the dojo—including Master Cha—on what they had learned during our training. I usually performed well on the belt tests because my parents had me practice the night before. They had me recite the taekwondo mantra before I was able to present my newly learned techniques. I advanced from yellow to green, to blue, to red, and to brown. But when it was time for me to get my red-and-black belt, which was considered the junior master belt, Master Cha thought that I wasn't ready. He said I hadn't fully mastered control, as I tended to get angry then things weren't going my way or when people disrespected me, so he postponed my belt exam.

With the master belt exam postponed, my mom thought that the best way to spend the weekend would be at Frost Valley YMCA to have some fun swimming, biking, and playing volleyball. My mom believed that the weekend at Frost Valley would not only cheer me up but also help me control myself. Having fun calmed my anger. The next weekend, I was able to attempt my junior master belt exam and succeeded.

Becoming a black belt was a challenge, as it was the highest of the belt ranking system. It was mostly adults, including Master Cha himself, who were black belts. The black belt is about more than just having control and discipline. It's about being an adult and a leader. The teacher of each class always has a black belt, and the other belts are the ones following their instructions. I was only twelve, and even though I mastered control and discipline, I was acting a bit immature.

So, for the next two years, I had to work hard in not only training but also being mature. When I was almost fourteen years old, I finally got my black belt. I was still young and had a lot to learn, but I guess Master Cha believed that I had fully mastered control and discipline and had earned the right of being a black belt. Putting on that black belt felt like I was at the top of my class, like I was finally able to achieve something in my life.

I was able to teach the class when Master Cha had to spend time in his office going over paperwork. Since I was the youngest black belt, I usually just led the class through the standard exercises, running around the dojo while jumping over a wooden stick and practicing moves with the stick. I felt that I was taking control of the class and working on my leadership skills.

As much as I loved my black belt status, I felt that I had more pressing matters to focus on, including schoolwork and having a normal, fourteen-year-old weekend. So, I told Master Cha that I was leaving the taekwondo dojo in order to pursue my life at school and home.

Throughout high school, I'd stop by Master Cha's and catch up a bit. Sometimes I just wish I could go back to the dojo and reflect on all of the times I spent there—learning new moves; practicing with wooden swords, staves, and nunchucks; and dueling with my fellow classmates. But in late May of 2018, Master Cha decided to retire as a taekwondo instructor. The dojo became a storage room for the dry cleaner next door. I haven't seen Master Cha since then, and I wish that I could see him one last time and thank him for all that he did for me.

The Christmas Tree Lighting Incident

When I was seven, we went to the big Christmas tree lighting ceremony near the train station in Ridgewood. Thousands of people crammed around a forty-foot Norway pine decorated with colored lights and tinsel. There were speeches and bands and songs and, for me, deafening noise and chaos. We were with another family, the DeZaios, who had two kids around Eliza's and my age. I think I either got bored or sick of the noise and wandered away from our group. By the time everyone realized I was missing, it became a scene from the movie *Home Alone*. Both sets of parents were panicked, thinking I might have been stolen or was alone, lost, and crying.

Little did they know that I had a better plan. Since everyone was outside listening to the *blah blah blah* of the ceremony, I snuck into the Häagen Dazs ice cream store I'd wandered to when I was three and had been to many times with my parents. There was no line and plenty of good service from my friend, the manager behind the counter. My order was simple: mango sorbet. I might not have had an expansive vocabulary, but I knew what kinds of food made me happy. When the search party finally found me after twenty minutes of panic, I was smiling and holding a cone of mango sorbet. The owner of Häagen Dazs said, "We know Sammy, and we know what he likes."

This is an example of why the town of Ridgewood was so important in my life. People knew me as the kid who couldn't really talk, so they looked out for me and took an interest in my well-being.

This year, I went to the Christmas tree lighting to find out what the experience was like as an adult. It was very different from the chaos of more than twenty years ago. Rather than seeing a bunch of rear ends and the bottoms of winter jackets, I was able to see above the mass of people crowding the streets. One can only imagine what it was like as a four-foot-something kid to be navigating a sea of bodies. But as an adult, I was able to maneuver my way around the town because I'm the big one at 6'7" while almost everyone else is a full head shorter than me. I thought about going into the Häa-gen Dazs and ordering the mango sorbet with rainbow sprinkles for old time's sake, but at twenty-eight years old, I no longer am keen on frozen confections when it is freezing outside.

Sammy's bravery is his greatest strength. It didn't matter if it was jumping off the highest point of a swing or sitting next to a lonely kid at school, he was always the kid who did what he felt was right or fun. He has always been the bolder, more adventurous sibling, while I was timid, afraid of what others would think or feel about my words and actions. My psychiatrist has said that it has to do with being more aware of what would trigger Sammy or Mom and Dad so they wouldn't worry too much. But I know it was because, at times, I was ashamed of how much I resented my best friend and the attention he got.

Truthfully, I didn't realize that Sammy wasn't "normal" until I was in middle school and saw that other kids' brothers weren't like Sammy. They didn't see specialists or go to special schools or get extra special attention from their parents. When I did take notice, I looked at how others treated him. It didn't take much—a conde-scending tone or look—and I went into protection/fix/hide it mode.

But Sammy never noticed, or if he did, he just didn't care. That was a lesson I should have taken note of.

It's not easy being the sibling of someone with disabilities. There are times you handle it well and times where you look like the most hateful, ungrateful person on the planet. But there are no guidebooks on how to handle feeling like an afterthought. I'm thankful that our parents did their best to treat us equally, even if we weren't. I am ashamed of how I treated Sammy in the past. I wasn't always the best sister or friend. But despite the previous negativity, I never regretted having Sammy in my life. He has changed me for the better. His attitude in life has inspired me to be more lenient with others (sometimes at a detriment to my own sanity), and to look past outward actions or appearances.

—Sister, Eliza Flood

Dude at the Ranch

During the summer of 2003, my nuclear family, along with my Uncle Dick, Aunt Jodie, cousins Hailey, Hugh, and Charlie, and Floodo and Sally all traveled to Jackson Hole, Wyoming. The trip was a celebration of Floodo and Sally's retirement from the Salisbury School, where Floodo had been the headmaster since 1988. They lived in a beautiful house at Salisbury with an ideal sledding hill among the many distractions for this rambunctious kid.

The Wyoming trip was a next-level experience for me. I had never seen mountains so tall or so much open space. We were guests at a dude ranch called Moosehead Ranch. I don't think the wranglers looked at me as a dude but rather as a quiet kid who loved to cause terror all over the property. Eliza was a horse lover as well as a dog lover, and all she could talk about was her horse and the experience of riding. I, on the other hand, was a bit scared of the huge animals and unsure how to control the beasts. Moosehead was the first place I rode a horse. His name was Wash Key, and he was brown, furred, and lazy. We would go for rides every day, and Wash Key would just pause and eat grass while the others rode on, making me fall behind during every ride. It didn't seem like a big deal at the time, but eventually it added some crazy drama to the trip.

One day, Mom left the ranch to pick Dad up at the airport, so we went for the ride with Floodo, Sally, and the ranchers. Wash Key chose that day to be a bit of a jerk. He bit the behind of Eliza's slow, fat, gray horse named Smokey. This caused Smokey to spook and run away with Eliza, who was trying to hang on for the wild ride. Wash Key decided to join the fun and chase Smokey as if we were in the Kentucky Derby. We held on for our dear lives, terrified, as the two horses raced across a two-lane highway. Fortunately, there were no cars in sight. Finally, as we reached a lake, one of the wranglers galloped to our rescue and saved us from our doom. My sister was sobbing uncontrollably after the whole episode, and apparently I kept saying, "I'm going to have a heart attack!" It's funny now, but my grandparents were the ones who were about to have heart attacks as they watched their two grandchildren almost get injured by runaway horses. After that fiasco, I was given a horse named Monty. He was a mellow black horse who did stop at times to eat grass, but he wasn't crazy or lazy like Wash Key.

I always wondered if that was how my parents felt when they were dealing with an out of control monster. The tables had turned, seeing as how I was stuck riding a horse that had a mind of its own and didn't want to follow directions, just the way I was when I was a kid.

I asked my parents why they decided to take me on the trip and put me in a dangerous spot with a crazy horse. They claimed they didn't know about the crazy horse but did know that they needed to keep pushing me into situations I was not familiar with. They wanted me to have a full childhood, wanted to make sure they challenged me with new experiences. As out of control as I could be, they never hid me from new experiences and opportunities. They were always pushing me to experience life and the bigger world. If I had just stayed in my home-to-school bubble, I would never have evolved and learned how to be part of society. It must not have been easy for them or me, but it worked.

Sammy might be the most agile and athletic kid I have ever seen. He could walk across the top of a swing set and jump down seven feet, sticking the landing and then walking away, ready to follow his curiosity to whatever might intrigue him.

When Sammy skied for the first time, he showed no fear, skipping the pizza form and going instead right to French fries. He would fly down the mountain loving the speed and looking for jumps. On our second day skiing, we rode the chair lift, and he pointed to kids going over a small jump and smiled. He didn't say a word. We exited the lift, and he French fried down the hill and over the jump. Of course, he stuck the landing and bombed to the end of the lift line. Clearly, athletic accomplishments and individual sports were fine, but the chaos of team sports was too much. Once I finally realized it was about his reality and not my expectations, I was amazed and could celebrate all his accomplishments.

—Dad, Sam Flood

My First Wild Spring Break

When I was in the fifth grade, in 2005, my family and I traveled to Miami and stayed in a hotel, a three-story, red-roofed building that looked out over a beach with white sand. The hotel also had a large swimming pool. But my favorite part of the hotel was the arcade where I played Street Fighter 2 as well as Metal Slug, two games that tested my hand–eye coordination and concentration. I met a couple of kids, Brian and Sophie, who lived in New York and were around my age. We talked about the animated show *Avatar: the Last Airbender* and what we had watched during the first season. My parents were a bit surprised and clearly thrilled that I was actually speaking with kids we'd just met. They saw this as a huge step forward for the now-talking Sammy. It was one more example of getting me out of the Ridgewood bubble and into new worlds that would challenge and engage me.

Movies and TV shows typically show crazy spring breaks, where college students party all night long, drink heavily, do drugs, start fights, and get involved in other reckless activities. Clearly I missed out on some of those wild times. But heck, as a fifth grader, talking about *Avatar* and other shows was pretty crazy for a guy who didn't speak until age five or six. That trip and every excursion we took was an opportunity for my family to take a break from our stressful daily routines. When Mom and Dad tell me about all the doctors, speech therapists, and specialists they used to take me to, I get a feeling the vacations meant a lot to them as well.

New Interests in Comics, Video Games and TV

I made many friends during my elementary school days, mainly guys. We played basketball, baseball, and football. We read comics, played video games, watched TV shows, and swam in the town swimming pool. We sometimes went to each other's birthday parties, mainly at bowling alleys, arcades, swimming pools, basketball courts, and pizza shops. I specifically remember one arcade called Fuddruckers that we went to before it turned into a mattress store. I miss that arcade. Taking part in birthday parties and hangout events with my fellow classmates made me feel like I belonged.

When I was between seven and ten years old, I was into comic books like *Batman, Teen Titans, Spider-Man, X-Men, Avengers, Transformers,* and *Star Wars.* I first started reading comics when I was seven. My parents took me to a comic bookstore downtown, where I saw a *Robin* comic and became immediately attached to the concept of comics. I was impressed by their way of presenting teenage life. I began to develop a taste for sci-fi adventure because of those comics, as well as some of the Saturday morning and Toonami shows I watched, like *Gundam, Power Rangers* (mainly *Time Force, Wild Force, Dino Thunder,* and *SPD*), *Outlaw Star, Zoids,* and *Transformers.*

I felt that life was a sci-fi adventure and that it was sometimes an anime adventure in a feudal Japanese setting, thanks to shows like *Ruroni Kenshin, Naruto, Samurai Jack,* and *Avatar: the Last Airbender.* The Japanese designs of both the settings and characters of these shows taught me a little about Japanese and Asian culture. I also really dug the music and fight scenes of these shows. For example, *Ruroni Kenshin* and *Samurai Jack* showed how samurai fought with all of the sword styles and quick movements. *Naruto* and *Avatar: the Last Airbender* used both magic and martial arts during their fight scenes as a way of presenting which character had a special ability as well as what kind of character trait they had.

It was a different world for me—the art, the characters—that I could enter whenever I wanted. It also provided the calm I needed to learn more control and discipline while having fun.

I also began to develop an interest in video games, mainly thanks to games like *Sly Cooper*, *Jak and Daxter*, *Sphinx and the Cursed Mummy*, and *Kingdom Hearts*. When I was nine years old, I got a PlayStation 2. My first two games were *Jak and Daxter* and *Sphinx and the Cursed Mummy*. Looking at the artwork of both covers for both games, I was impressed by their designs. When I popped the CDs into the console, I was also amazed by the music of *Jak and Daxter* as well as the Egyptian theme of *Sphinx and the Cursed Mummy*. Those and similar games took me into another world. I was never good at those games when I was in elementary school because I was just learning how to play them. Over time, I learned how to master them, thanks to the same control and discipline that earned me a black belt.

Time and Memory

One of the things you should know about me is that I am super organized and have a place for everything. My learning differences make me the last guy to ever misplace anything. In my world, everything has its place, and I always maintain structure for my belongings and my life in general. If Mom says we are going to the store at 10 A.M., I am in the car at 10 A.M. waiting for her. She has learned not to look around the house for me since a plan is a plan.

I also have a memory that lets me recount entire conversations going back ten or even twenty years. This special gift gives me the structure and organization I need to be successful. It also frustrates my parents since I'm always saying things like: "Do you remember when you confiscated my comic books when I was ten?"

Dad will then say, "Sorry I ruined your life," and laugh.

I would explain to my dad that a teacher had said I kept talking about my comic books and started using phrases from them.

Dad has no memory of that incident, but I can recount the entire conversation. That is how detailed my memory is. My dad says it is like I have the entire movie of my life hidden in my brain.

Not the Real Housewives of New Jersey

For most of my life, I spent lots of time with Mom's side of the family, which consists of her older sisters, Kathryn and Pat, and her older brother, Kevin.

Mom's parents, John and Pat Cahill, lived fifteen minutes from us in Franklin Lakes, New Jersey. If you happen to watch Mom's favorite channel, Bravo, you might have caught a glimpse of Franklin Lakes. One of the *Real Housewives of New Jersey* lived in the town, but I promise you that neither my grandmother nor aunts were on that show.

My maternal grandfather, Papa, died when I was very young, so I didn't get to know him very well. But I am sure he never forgot the weekend I spent with him when I was eighteen months old. My parents and Eliza went to a wedding in Seattle, and they left the wild child in Franklin Lakes. One afternoon, my grandparents put me down for a nap in my portable crib. They were thrilled that there was no noise from the room for almost three hours. Little did they know that I had decided to redecorate the walls in their guest bedroom. I was able to find a loose piece of wallpaper and ripped sections from the wall, piece by piece. When they finally decided to check on me, the room was missing an entire wall of paper. I think that gave them an idea of the crazy antics that my mom had to deal with twenty-four hours a day. Until that point, I'm not sure they believed how much damage an eighteen-month-old kid could cause.

Aunt Kathryn and Aunt Pat used to live in Franklin Lakes, and Uncle Kevin lived in Leonia, a town close to one of the highways that leads to New York City. Because our families lived close to one another, my aunts and uncle spent holidays at each other's houses.

We have a Christmas Eve tradition where we open each other's gifts after having roast beef for dinner. With our cousins Allyson and Sydney, the daughters of Aunt Kathryn and around my age, as well as Briana and Clarissa, daughters of Uncle Kevin and younger than me, we spent our Christmas Eve watching holiday specials like *How the Grinch Stole Christmas*, *Elf* (starring Will Ferrell), and *Love Actually* while the adults drank and laughed at funny stories from their past.

Escaping with The Flood Family to Rhode Island

I love spending time with my family, and we've had plenty of fun vacations together. We often went to Jamestown, Rhode Island, to Floodo and Sally's summer home.

In Rhode Island, I get to devote time to my dad's side of the family, including my cousins Hailey, Hugh, and Charlie Flood, the children of my dad's older brother, Dick, as well as my cousins John and Caroline Fritz, who are the children of my dad's younger sister, Kassy. We spend most of our time swimming on the beaches, exploring the hiking trails of Beavertail Park, which has a lighthouse at the northern end of the island, and exploring the nearby town of Newport. There's an arcade in Newport filled with all kinds of video games. For a ten year old, it seemed amazing, bigger than life. Now, when I walk by the building, it looks small because it is a one-floor building that usually gets crammed during the summer.

The world, and specifically my world, looked so much different back when I was young. I needed places to escape from all of the stress from school and family. I needed Sammy Time. The arcade allowed me to enter new worlds and block out everyone else, such as members of my family as well as the people in the arcade. As I look back, I see that I clearly needed a lot of stimulation to keep me engaged. Thankfully, I have matured and can now occupy my time with a good book or banging on the keyboard writing stories. Some of the fantasy stories I write might be rooted in the old games I played at the Newport arcade.

We didn't have a summer home of our own between 2003 and 2006, so we rented a house in Jamestown every year. One summer, we were in a huge house with a TV in almost every bedroom. I was so happy that I had a TV in my room. At home in New Jersey, my parents wouldn't let me have my own TV since they believed it would distract me while I was doing homework. But, at this rental, Eliza was given the room with a TV from the 1970s, and it played only three channels. So, she came into my room to watch her programs. Usually, the big sister controlled the TV, but that time, since the good TV was in my room, I got to make the "critical" decisions about what we would watch. It was fun to have a little bit of control over something as simple as TV shows. It was one more lesson on making sure I could have a say in life and the decisions people were making about me most of the time.

The Family Dog

When I was seven years old, my dad brought us a basset hound puppy he got from New York City on his way home from work one day. Eliza really loved dogs and decided to keep him for herself.

While the whole family was excited to have a dog of our own, we had a little difficulty trying to come up with a name for him. I suggested that we named our puppy Dino, like the dinosaur from *The Flintstones*, but nobody wanted to name our dog after a cartoon character. Eliza decided to name him Marco Polo, because she was doing a history project about Marco Polo and how he traveled across the Middle East and to China through the Silk Road. There's also an Asian restaurant named Marco Polo in Glen Rock, the town next to Ridgewood.

Keeping a dog was great, but raising him was a challenge. Marco Polo would just make a mess of things as he used our living room as his bathroom. Mom was furious that she had to clean up after Marco's messes. Sometimes Dad would call Marco "Dumb Dog." Most of the time, we had to take him out for walks whenever he needed it. I took Marco out a few times. While it is fun walking a dog, the worst part is that I have to pick up his number two using a newspaper bag, which is really disgusting when you think about it.

Marco could also get rather jumpy at times. One time when I was nine, there was this guy that Mom called to check some things in our house like the floors of our first floor. My parents told me not to let him in because Marco would jump on anyone who would knock on the front door. One morning, the floor specialist started knocking on our door. I decided to let him in because it was the right thing to do. But when I opened the door, Marco came charging in and jumped on the guy. He was licking him all over and clawing at him with his paws. My parents rushed toward the front door and backed Marco away from the floor specialist. Mom apologized to the guy about her dog as Dad dragged Marco away from him. Hours later, my parents scolded me for opening the door, which allowed Marco to jump all over the floor specialist. I guess the lesson learned here is that maybe I should be more careful of my surroundings whenever I let people in.

In another incident, Marco assaulted a woman. It all started when my mom, sister, and I were talking Marco for a walk through the neighborhood on a nice autumn day. We came across a brown-haired woman who was walking with her elderly mother. The old lady was fascinated by our dog and said he was cute. I decided to walk back home because I didn't want to be part of the conversation between my mom and the old woman. As I was about to walk away, the brown-haired woman said, "Your dog scratched my mom. Can we please use your phone?"

The elderly woman was bleeding from her hand. Not really knowing what happened, I escorted them back to my house.

The younger woman used our house phone and called 911. She said that Marco attacked her mom and that she needed medical attention. Moments later, ambulances were parked right outside of our house as some of the first responders were tending to the old lady. Some police officers asked the woman what really happened. The woman explained that her mother tried to pet our dog, but he scratched her hand. She also said that Marco needed to be put down for such an offense.

My mom argued that the woman's mother tried to pet Marco without her permission and she was getting a little too close to his personal space. My mom and the woman argued for what seemed like hours.

The police officers and emergency responders must have felt it was taking up too much of their day and decided to drive away.

We were thankful that the police didn't press any changes against us or Marco because they knew that it was just a big misunderstanding and we did nothing wrong. Mom knew that woman was looking to take our insurance money, as she was willing to sue us for what Marco did.

Despite these incidents, Marco was a fun dog to have and a great member of our family. He would always keep me company whenever Mom and Dad would go out at night. Marco would always hang out with Eliza and me whenever we watched TV, and he was great at playing catch in the backyard. Marco would also help Mom deal with her woodchuck problem, as the woodchucks would devour her plants. Marco Polo would act as the sole defender of the family's garden as he charged at any woodchuck who popped out of a hole to raid Mom's flowers and attack them. The woodchucks were scared by how vicious and big Marco is and fled in terror.

Marco may have been a "Dumb Dog" to Dad, but he was still a member of the Flood family, just like all dogs and cats who are owned by families around the world.

LIFE LESSONS

Be creative.

People are full of surprises.

A little control means a lot.

Chapter 3:
Tween Years from Twelve to Fifteen
(2006–2009)

Learning to Adjust to a Private School Setting

After I graduated from the Orchard School, my parents enrolled me in a private school called Eagle Hill in Greenwich, Connecticut. They sent me to Eagle Hill when I was about to enter sixth grade because they believed the Ridgewood school, Washington Middle School, wasn't prepared to help people like me. It was geared toward people who didn't have my kind of learning disabilities. Dr. Lifechanger had suggested that I go to Eagle Hill. If I attended Washington Middle School, she said, I would be in a self-contained classroom the way I was during my kindergarten years, meaning I would be backtracking.

> The plan for Sammy to attend Eagle Hill was complicated and expensive. We knew putting Sammy back into a self-contained classroom for sixth grade would crush his spirit and limit his development. He

needed role models who showed him how to behave and how to evolve as a middle schooler.

Eagle Hill has the reputation as the Harvard University for learning disabled children. Not surprisingly, it also cost more than Harvard but was worth every dollar. The process to get Sammy eligible and accepted was complicated. He spent two summers at the school proving he could handle the educational expectations. His fourth grade summer set the table and made his parents believe he belonged at Eagle Hill.

—Dad, Sam Flood

To see if I was ready for their program, Eagle Hill asked me to attend their summer school, where I could get to know the teachers better. At first, I didn't enjoy going to a summer school because, like most kids my age, I believed that it would be a drag to go to school during the summer. But over time, I enjoyed most of the classes such as literature, math, and writing, and they lasted only a half day, with no homework. We even had a beach day, when we all sailed to an island in Long Island Sound. The only negative about the summer school was that my mother had to drive through traffic forty-five or more minutes just to get me there.

The road from that first summer to Sammy's acceptance was much more complicated. After good reviews from the first summer, we were encouraged to have Sammy apply for acceptance for the fall of 2006. The interview and tour seemed to go well. The head of admissions spoke with Sammy about being on the basketball team and what it would be like to play on the various teams. She was also very encouraging about the entire package for him, even using the phrase "next year when you are at the school." Heading home that night, we felt confident that in a few weeks, the thick letter would arrive indicating Sammy had been accepted.

Unfortunately, there is never a straight line or easy path in the learning disability space. Apparently, the academic dean of Eagle Hill didn't feel Sammy could handle the work or program at the school. We were stunned, frustrated, and confused. Once again, we faced a road block, and once again, we turned to my father.

As the headmaster at Salisbury School, he knew the Eagle Hill Head of School, Mark Griffin. The call went through headmaster to headmaster to discuss Sammy's rejection and the process that led to that decision. Following the conversation, the door opened, and the school agreed that Sammy would attend another year of summer school and then have one academic year to prove he could succeed at Eagle Hill.

All we wanted was a chance for Sammy to show how smart he is and for the school to help unlock all that was trapped inside by his language processing issues. The conflicts with roommates and other students were always frustrating but did show he was trying to find his way in the community.

Jane again made the biggest sacrifice to make the Eagle Hill years work. She drove the eighty-two miles round trip across the old Tappan Zee Bridge two times a day, logging one hundred sixty-four miles a day and eight hundred twenty miles a week.

—Dad, Sam Flood

Once sixth grade arrived and it was time to attend Eagle Hill, I didn't like the idea of having to leave Ridgewood, away from my Orchid School friends. But my parents felt that Eagle Hill was the right place for me because it was a private school and it would help me learn how to master my learning disabilities.

Eagle Hill is a boarding school with two hundred students. It is located in the center of Greenwich and goes from sixth through ninth grade. The kids who attend the school have learning disabilities like mine. When I arrived, I was placed in a room with a fifteen-year-old boy named Sam (we'll learn more about Sam later in this chapter) from New York City. The schedule each day started with breakfast at 7:30 A.M., classes at 9 A.M., and in the afternoon, we were required to do some sport activities such as basketball, cross country, hockey, lacrosse, and baseball. Throughout the day, we had juice breaks and lunch breaks to give us a bit of free time in between classes. We did homework after sports as a way of wrapping up our day.

My Eagle Hill Classes

The classes I took were a bit tough at first, but I got the hang of things over time. My academic schedule included tutorial, literature, math, writing, science, art, and history.

My day typically began with a tutorial. After my homeroom, which ran from 8:30 A.M. to 9:30 A.M., I would go to Mrs. Reed's classroom. The other students were Matthew, a tall guy with red hair, and Jake, a short blond who was always faster than me in races during cross country. Mrs. Reed began each class with a few questions (such as "When did World War II end?") to warm us up for the day's lesson. After we answered her questions, Mrs. Reed had us work on an assignment, either something based on literature, like *The Last of the Mohicans, Treasure Island*, or *Dr. Jekyll and Mr. Hyde*, or an assignment based on a historic event recounted in a news magazine. I personally found tutorial to be the most basic of the classes I took in Eagle Hill. Maybe it was because Mrs. Reed just had us work on assignments that were more suited for literature or history. But some of the assignments were a bit fun, like the time when I was doing a book report on *Last of the Mohicans*. I had to use Lego characters to do a reenactment of one of the battle scenes in the book.

During the second period, I took literature, which was taught by Mrs. Clifford. After our tutorial class ended, Matthew and I would go to Mrs. Clifford's class in the building with the art studio. We read such books as *The Castle in the Attic*, *Shadow Children*, and ones about Sherlock Holmes. At first I thought that literature was my least favorite because Mrs. Clifford and I didn't see eye to eye. I either failed whatever homework assignment she gave me or I spoke out of line during a lecture. One time, Mrs. Clifford was giving a lecture, and I wasn't paying attention. When she asked me a question about what she was discussing, I asked Mrs. Clifford to repeat the question, which angered her. That made me realize that I should pay more attention instead of dozing off. She sent me to the headmaster's office as punishment for my lack of focus. Even though I had my problems with Mrs. Clifford, I enjoyed some of the books we read.

The third class was math, which was taught by Mrs. Pagel in the same building as the headmaster's office. Mrs. Pagel started class with basic math problems before we moved to learning some math equations. Most of these were based on fractions, decimals, and prices in everyday life, like paying for groceries. I was good at math because I could easily figure out the answers in my head or by drawing the problem on paper. From Mrs. Pagel's point of view, I was one of her favorite students mainly because I was good at math and solving problems. During one assignment, I created a scenario in which my parents were at a restaurant so I could add up how much they were spending for the meal. Mrs. Pagel was impressed that I used my mind and figured out how these price-related math problems should be done by roleplaying.

After a break, I headed to earth science, which was in the building that also had the gym. Mr. Moore taught us a lot about the earth as well as some of the planets that orbit the sun. Earth science was my least favorite class. I wasn't interested in the earth's plates and rotations. Also, Mr. Moore came off as hyperactive, always pressuring us with questions while we were trying to keep up with what he was explaining. With my ADHD, I found it difficult to stay focused on what he was teaching, so I had to owe him a lot of breaks. While my fellow classmates had free time outside of the library, I had to go to his office and just sit there for the entire break until the bell rang. But then I learned that I shouldn't goof off by drawing pictures of creatures in my notebook and instead focus and pay attention.

> Academically, Sammy seemed to thrive and always exceeded expectations. Because he struggled when he spoke, people underestimated his intellect. In some ways, it was the reverse of my academic situation. A college professor once said he wished I could write as well as I talked. With a keyboard in front of him, Sammy can bang out wonderful creative stories. The gift of a computer and a word processor opened the world to Sammy's humor and ability to tell stories.
> —**Dad, Sam Flood**

After earth science, I headed to my writing class with Mrs. Respecto. That is where I began to learn how to use a computer to write stories. Most of my stories have been deleted, but they were just childish fan fiction stories with poor sentence and story structure. Also, my Macbook died, and I couldn't recover the files. There were a few downsides to writing class. Mrs. Respecto had to restrict my writing choices in terms of dialogue and choice of words. From playing video games and watching TV, I had picked up a lot of adult themes. But because Eagle Hill is a school for all ages, I was forbidden to add swear words to my written work, and I had to avoid writing about sex or gory violence. We weren't allowed to write "making out" or "made out" because the teachers believed that making out was inappropriate.

The final class before study hall was history with Mr. Stern. He usually taught us about U. S. history and how the country came to be. We also learned some European history. Out of all of the classes, history was my favorite. Every Wednesday, Mr. Stern would show us a movie about historic events, such as the building of the Egyptian Pyramids and the Crusades.

We also had art class every Tuesday or Friday. Our art teacher, Mrs. Maida, taught us not only how to paint but also how to make other forms of art such as sketches and pottery. When Mrs. Maida showed us how to make things out of clay, I made a creature, and she was impressed. Just for the fun of it, I made more clay creatures, some resembling birds, snakes, fish, bulls, boars, and hounds. Mrs. Maida was so impressed that she let me take them back home.

My Sport Life

In the afternoon of that first fall, I ran cross country with fifteen or twenty other kids. We had to stretch before we ran. After the stretching, Mrs. DeLisle, our coach, had us run around the school. Sometimes, we had to run up and down a hill right next to the Eagle Hill entrance. At first, I liked cross country because we were running around the area as well as new locations in Greenwich County. But later on, I began to dislike cross country because I would always get winded. Mrs. DeLisle believed that I was out of shape, which was why I was always exhausted after every practice and meet. But I believed that she was burning up our energy by ordering the team to start each match by sprinting instead of jogging. Even though I didn't really enjoy cross country, I ran all fall, finishing each race in last place.

During the Eagle Hill winters, I signed up to play for the school basketball team, which was coached by Mr. Hanrahan. I was actually one of the best players of the Eagle Hill basketball team because of my height and skills on the court. During our first session after school, Coach Hanrahan taught me, along with my fellow teammates, the basics of basketball such as dribbling, passing, and shooting two- and three-pointers. Each day, we warmed up by running around the gym and practicing our shots. After that, we practiced a few more skills such as shooting three pointers, passing, and sprinting from one end of the court to another. Basketball practices usually ended with either a practice scrimmage before a game or a little practice shooting before we hit the showers and got some homework done during study hall.

As the star player of the Eagle Hill Basketball team, I was the trump card to winning most of our games, if I was called up from the bench. Sure, the team had lost some games in the past, but we got better as we worked harder than ever to win the games we played.

Being a part of a basketball team meant we got to play a few games against teams from other schools in Greenwich County. Most of the games took place at the Eagle Hill gym, while the rest were at other schools. One time, our school competed in a basketball game at a school called St. Andrews. I wasn't huge on playing basketball games at other schools because I worried I might not have enough time to do my homework, but I liked traveling to new schools. Sometimes we'd go out for a well-earned snack at the nearest Dunkin Donuts or Pizza Hut. Some were a bit nicer looking than Eagle Hill, with big and exotic buildings.

His basketball tales sound like an old timer reminiscing about his starring role on the court "back in the day." The reality was Sammy was the tallest kid on the court but far from the star of the team. He tended to accumulate fouls with his long arms drawing the ref's whistle. One time when an offensive foul was called, Sammy looked down at his jersey number and realized he was the offending party. He went over to the ref and apologized, saying he was sorry; meanwhile, the opposing team had already in-bounded the ball and was racing up the court.

The basketball coach was always supportive and kind toward Sammy. One game, the big guy scored eight points and was on cloud nine for a week. He could always shoot the ball above the arms of the smaller opponents, so rebounds and put backs worked well for the dude. The chaos on the court was not ideal for Sammy, but the coach simplified the game so Sammy knew his place was down low in the post.

—Dad, Sam Flood

For my spring sport, I decided to join the Eagle Hill baseball team. Some of my fellow classmates such as Max, John, Casey, and Dillon played baseball. My science teacher, Mr. Moore, coached the team. When I first started playing baseball, my parents took me to a coach in Midland Park near Ridgewood so I could get good at hitting and catching the ball. After class, my teammates and I would put on our baseball uniforms and head over to the field behind the school for a little catching before baseball practice truly began.

We'd warm up with a few laps around the diamond and then started practicing our pitches. Later, we sprinted across the field as we threw the ball back and forth until we reached the other side. We ended each session with a practice game as a way of prepping for our next baseball game against another school. Our games against rival baseball teams from other schools usually had us travel around Greenwich County. I only hit the ball a few times, but I was a good catcher, and I could throw the ball to another teammate to get a player out.

My Eagle Hill Social Life

I wasn't too thrilled about transferring to Eagle Hill because I had to leave my old friends behind. But over time, I made some new friends, like Dash, who was tall and had dark curly hair and was known for being friendly with everyone; and John, who wore glasses, had shaved blond hair and was a bit pale. He was known for being smart. Max was muscular and had blond hair shaped in a bowl cut. He was known for being a star hockey player in our school. Matthew had red hair and went to many classes with me, and Dillon, who had hair that was a mix between brown and red, hung out a lot with me in the dorm common area. Casey was chubby and had long black hair that made him look like one of those musicians in emo rock bands. We had some similar interests, such as anime, video games, TV shows, and movies. I also became friends with some of the dorm teachers such as Mr. DeLisle, Mr. Combs, and my advisor as well as my math teacher, Mr. Flood (no relation), my gym teacher, Mr. Hans, my art teacher, Mrs. Maida, and writing teacher, Mrs. Pagel.

I did get myself into some trouble often at Eagle Hill, mainly because I got into people's personal space and put my hands on them. One time I was waiting with my sixth grade math class outside of Mrs. Pagel's classroom. I got a little close to a fellow classmate of mine named Tiana. She said I was hovering over her and told me, "You're in my personal space."

Suddenly my speech teacher, Mrs. Chase-Karel, walked in and told me to back away from her. Mrs. Chase-Karel also told me everyone at Eagle Hill has a personal bubble, an imaginary barrier to prevent students from touching each other.

After Mrs. Chase-Karel left the scene, the other students ganged up on me and said that I was in their personal bubble. Eagle Hill had a no-touch policy, and anyone who touched another person would be punished by having to sit in a corner.

I would also get in trouble sometimes when I lost focus in class or did not complete my homework. I would owe juice break or lunch break, which meant that instead of having a break, I would have to do detention. I didn't like to owe juice or lunch break at times because I would be separated from my peers. But the breaks gave me time to do some homework.

My Disastrous First Roommate

I had some problems with my first roommate, Sam. I used to call him Sternie just so other people could tell us apart. Sternie would whine and complain about the nickname and just about every other thing I did. For example, whenever I tried to get on his bed or change my clothes on my bed, Sam would whine. He also drank all of my Pediasure milk, which my parents provided to help me grow strong. So, Mr. and Mrs. DeLisle, the dorm proctors, decided that my Pediasure drinks should remain in Mrs. DeLisle's office.

Sam believed that whoever his roommate was should think the same way he did. He should have known that he didn't have a right to dictate what I wore, for example. I knew that I shouldn't let my roommate dictate my actions. Sometimes the best way to grow up is to not let people push you around.

The Kicking Incident

One time I kicked Kathlyn, a thirteen-year-old student in my literature class, in the school library. The problem started when two other students, Emily and Kevin, told me that I was sitting in their seat.

"What are you doing here? These are our seats," Kevin said.

"Trying to do my homework here, thank you very little," I replied.

They didn't care and still demanded that I get off my seat, which resulted in arguing.

Kathlyn got involved and said, "You can't speak to my friends like that."

I told her to stay out of it, but she didn't listen. Like a stubborn mule, she kept on yelling and arguing.

I couldn't take it anymore. I kicked her so hard, she flew toward a stand of books that tumbled off of the shelf and landed on her.

Mrs. Sweeney, one of Kathlyn's teachers, entered and saw her student crying. She asked us what had just happened.

Emily and Kevin pointed their fingers at me.

I was sent to Mr. Breakell, who taught a class in the library.

Emily and Kevin told their side of what happened, and Mr. Breakell told me that I had to be punished for it by owing lunch break.

I tried to do some homework while I was owing lunch break, but another teacher, Mrs. DiPalma, entered my detention room and asked, "What are you doing?"

I replied, "I'm trying to do my homework."

She told me I was not allowed to because I was being punished.

I argued with Mrs. DiPalma until she had had enough, and she sent me to Headmaster Griffin's office. I told him my side of the story, and he said that he would talk to these students about the fact they have no right to own seats, and he would talk to Kathlyn and tell her that she can't get herself involved in anyone else's business but her own, and he let me out of my detention.

The incident taught me that I shouldn't physically hurt other people, even when they aren't listening to me. The kicking incident could have been avoided if I just chose a different seat.

An Interest in Games and Shows

At Eagle Hill, I continued to spend free time playing video games and watching TV shows. Through the games, I viewed the world as some ancient Mediterranean adventure, with me going on seafaring quests, slaying monsters, and exploring the wondrous sites.

I also began to develop an interest in fantasy series, mainly *The Lord of the Rings*. I enjoyed the stories of hobbits, elves, dwarves, orcs, and other fantasy adventure characters. Fantasy is how I viewed the world, and it was my escape from the issues I faced in school, the bothersome people I had to deal with, and all of the stress I had to go through on a daily basis. I knew that I wanted to write a story of my own at some point.

I watched anime, and shows such as *Bleach, Full Metal Alchemist, Family Guy*, and *South Park* taught me how to swear. Eagle Hill didn't approve because those words were inappropriate for the younger students. But the words helped fuel my creativity in writing.

One time, I was quoting an episode from *Family Guy* where Lois and Peter, the main characters, are naked on a couch after getting high. Lois said, "He's knocking on the back door. Should I let him in?"

Most of the students who heard me say this, mainly young kids, were confused and said that what I quoted made them feel like they're gay, which made no sense whatsoever. But then I learned that the younger students don't fully understand a lot of the adult concepts in the shows I enjoyed. Later on, I found out the term "back door" has an explicit sexual meaning.

Another time, when my class and I were doing homework during study hall, a younger student caught me looking at a *South Park* website. A little while later, the woman proctoring study hall caught me as well and asked, "How do you think it makes me feel when you're looking up websites on mature rated shows like *Family Guy* and *South Park*?" So, she banned me from using my computer during study hall. But I had an assignment I needed to complete for literature class. I felt that it was my fault for looking up information on the internet and becoming distracted by those shows when I should have been doing my homework, but part of me felt that the kid who was in my study hall should have kept his mouth shut and not snitched on me.

Marco Polo

Marco Polo died during my last year at Eagle Hill. Marco had cancer, and he wasn't getting any better, so my mom and I took him to the vet. When we got him there, the vet told my mom that there was nothing they could do for Marco, and they suggested he be put to sleep. That was the first time I saw my mom cry, and when she told dad about it on the phone, that was the first time I heard him cry. The next day, my mom and I went to Millbrook, a boarding school in New York State Eliza attended.

When Eliza and I were waiting outside of the dorm while mom was in the bathroom, she turned to me and said, "Hey, Sam, you've gotten taller."

I replied, "Hey, Eliza, Marco's dead." I hugged her, but she freed herself and ran into the dorm sobbing. After Mom calmed Eliza down, we drove back home so she could recover from the death of her dog.

This incident has been told several times by the family. Although Eliza likes to tell her side of the story and portrays me as some kind of idiotic sadist, I try to tell my side of the story of how Dad called me and said that when Eliza was told the news of Marco's death, I should hug her. I would also like to point out that telling Eliza about Marco was Mom's stupid idea because she was the one who drove me to Millbrook that day even though I could have stayed home. But Mom says that she could not leave me alone in the house since I was young. Even though I was fifteen at the time, I wasn't old enough to stay at the house by myself.

History has a habit of repeating itself because in 2011, when my Aunt Pat died of alcohol poisoning, my dad decided to take me to Millbrook to tell Eliza about Aunt Pat's passing. By that time, Eliza was a member of the women's hockey team, and she had just lost a game. I went over to Eliza and said, "I'm sorry about your loss."

Dad panicked and rushed to silence me in front of Eliza, but I learned from my mistake and added, "About the game."

After Eliza changed into her normal attire, Dad told her about Aunt Pat dying, and I felt that I should have stayed home. But Mom was probably busy dealing with Aunt Pat's funeral arrangements, and Dad felt that I shouldn't be home alone, even though I was seventeen then and was old enough to take care of myself. Maybe Mom should have told Dad to let me hang at home while he told Eliza about Aunt Pat's passing. The important thing is that my mom and dad told me that I need to keep my mouth shut at certain times mainly because sometimes things are better thought than said.

Proving Myself

At Eagle Hill, I always had to prove myself in order to move forward in life. I had to go to two summer programs in order to show the teachers that I am a capable student. I always had to push myself so people could see that I was willing to be a dedicated student. But what occurred after Eagle Hill wasn't a step in the right direction. It turned out to be a step backward because of what I was about to learn and experience in the next school I attended, Maplebrook.

LIFE LESSONS

Find the bright side of a situation.

Being a star means finding the right place.

Good communication can prevent bad incidents.

Some things are better thought than said.

Chapter 4:

First Year of High School, a.k.a. the Worst Year of My Life

(2010)

After graduating eighth grade from Eagle Hill School, I went to Maplebrook, a private school in New York State. How did I end up at Maplebrook? Well, after interviewing at multiple schools similar to Eagle Hill, I never received the thick envelope indicating acceptance. The thin envelopes contained letters saying that they did not have enough room for me or did not have the right means to support a student like me with my specific learning disabilities.

My dad told me that I yawned a lot during my school interviews, which might be a reason why schools did not accept me. In one interview, I jumped up more than once and excused myself to the bathroom. Apparently, I was very stressed for the interview. My yawns and bathroom breaks were a clear indication that the strain of the process was preventing me from interviewing well, even though I had prepared. I did practice interviews. Mom or

Dad would play the admissions officers, and it was easy when they were the people asking the questions. But the nerves would hit when I met with a person I did not know. Dad reminded me, "You gotta be ready for the big games." But these interviews were not games and did not open any educational doors for me.

In the end, only Maplebrook accepted me, and part of me felt that the school just needed more students. We had driven by the school for years as we drove from New Jersey to my grandparents' house in Salisbury, Connecticut. In retrospect, I wish we had learned more about the school and the students. I am partially responsible for the rocky year since my behavior was not ideal. But the atmosphere at the school and the lack of leadership from teachers created a *Lord of the Flies* vibe. A small group of kids were bullies and ran the dorms. My dorm master was a troubled man and ended up stealing from the students.

It was clear that I was one of the more advanced students academically. I could do the work in my sleep. Eagle Hill had prepared me for more complex topics from math to writing. So with no challenge in the classroom and navigating the bullies, it was a rough year. Eagle Hill had always pushed me academically to achieve more. Maplebrook's teachers seemed to just barely do anything to help kids improve.

Insulting my Intelligence

In English class, I felt what we covered was the same material I had already learned in elementary school. So I goofed around a lot, mostly playing on my laptop. My dad made the situation worse by telling me to stay focused, which felt impossible with the easy material. For example, one English teacher gave us an assignment to fill in sentences with the words listed on the bottom of the page, sort of like a crossword puzzle. The questions and answers were at an elementary school level.

Typing class also made me feel as if I was taking a few steps backward because I had learned how to type back in elementary school. But whenever I approached the teacher, she thought I was talking back to her, and she sent me out of the classroom. Some of these "arguments" were my fault, but she, like the rest of the Maplebrook teachers, was not strong at her job, which is helping students like me who have learning disabilities.

Math class was bad for a few reasons. We covered the same topics, like dividing, multiplying, and adding fractions, that I had already learned at Eagle Hill. And sometimes, we did not learn at all; the math teacher just had us watching reruns of *Monk* on his laptop. I also felt he was a bit of a creep. One time when we were watching *Transformers, Revenge of the Fallen*, he said, "I wish I was Megan Fox's underwear." It made me realize some of the teachers in that godforsaken school were lowlifes.

Health class was not much better; the teacher just taught us about the human body, which I'd already learned about at the Orchard School. I also never got along with most of the students in that class. I felt that my intelligence was being insulted when one of the students, Suzanne, gave me a booklet about puberty. Eventually, the health class teacher decided to transfer me to a history class. And thank God, because I could not take another second of relearning about the human circulatory system.

How I Was Treated

The students at Maplebrook called me a freak, a weirdo, a loser, and other hurtful names. They also picked fights with me and accused me of being the one who started the fights whenever there was trouble. Some of the students told me not to swear so much.

As the school year went on, I realized that those students did not like me and wanted me to get into trouble. Or they did not like to hear the sound of my voice because they thought it was "annoying." They also felt they had a right to mooch off of me by using my laptop to do whatever they needed. Part of me wanted to tell them, "Get your own laptop, mooch." But it was partly my fault because I'd been part of some incidents when I could have walked away.

For example, one of the students, Josh, tricked me into unplugging the TV in the girls' common area so he could recharge his laptop. I could have told him no and that he should do it himself, but he pretended to be my friend and offered me money in return. I unplugged the TV, and most of the girls hated me for ruining their show.

> We knew there were issues at Maplebrook and regretted sending Sammy to the school. Clearly this experience scarred Sammy and had a deep impact on him. The huge lesson for us was to be present and to question everything. We did attend parents weekends and sporting events and went to dinners, but clearly we needed to register a more regular cadence with the school. After fighting to get him admitted to the most appropriate schools and presenting him with the most suitable opportunities, for the first time in Sammy's life, we ended up sending him down the wrong path.
> —Dad, Sam Flood

Anti-Bullying

Two students, Jason and Peter, would accuse me of looking up porn while we were doing homework, even though I was not. They would keep harassing me. Over and over again, they said,

"Stop looking up porn." One time, Jason said, "I am going to cut out your tongue because I cannot stand the sound of your voice." I remember when an anti-bullying group came to Maplebrook. The spokesperson asked me about what I was going through. I told him that I had a hard time when accused of looking at porn while doing homework in the library. Pete made up a false story of how I had bullied him, saying I had beaten him up for his money. But he made the error of adding my name when really he should not have. The anti-bullying spokesperson told the students never to reveal the names of the people bullying them. My mom told me that the reason Jason and Peter were harassing me was that they were using me as a scapegoat because they were looking at porn and blaming me.

"A Child"

Mikhela, a Jamaican student with black braided hair, treated me badly by calling me a child and serving me last whenever she handed out ice cream after a meal. "You interrupted me while I was doing homework in the library," she said one time when I was in line for dessert. I could not understand why she would be angry at me for something that wasn't my fault and something she could have easily ignored.

Your Head, not Your Hands: Fall 2009

One kid named Yaya, a sixteen-year-old Moroccan student in the tenth grade, treated me badly mainly because he was just following his friend, John, who acted mean toward me because I stared at him a lot. One time, Yaya kicked me in the groin while we were in the locker room after basketball practice. He was just goofing around, but I felt he had some sort of grudge against me. A few days later, I was wandering around the campus after we had completed our homework. I walked up to Yaya and his friends and told him, "What you did was wrong."

He shouted back, "You are annoying, and no one likes you."

I suddenly felt angry. "You hate America; you're like the terrorists." It was a line I'd heard on *Family Guy*.

My comment resulted in a fight, and at one point, I head butted him.

Yaya fell down, crying loudly.

Suddenly a group of students surrounded me and yelled at me for what I did.

The day after that fight, I was suspended for three days and had to go home. My mom got into an argument with the headmistress of the school, Mrs. Scully, who downplayed Yaya's actions of kicking me in the groin. When Mrs. Scully proclaimed that what I did was wrong, my mom shot back at her, saying that Yaya was wrong for kicking me, and that I did not use my hands to hurt him.

Even after that incident, Yaya was always looking for fights with me even though the whole headbutting incident was behind us. Looking back, I believe that Yaya, like a few others, had violent tendencies, mainly toward me.

Throwing Books at Girls: Winter 2009

I got into another incident with Victoria, a girl in my class who was short, wore glasses, and had long, curly blonde hair. During breakfast one morning, I had gotten into an argument with Ester, a Spanish girl, and Victoria told me to knock it off.

In a profanity-laden missive, I insulted both Ester and Victoria.

"I'm telling a teacher because what you just said is inexcusable," she shouted.

Imitating Stewie Griffin from *Family Guy*, I repeated what I'd said. Victoria was angry and stormed off to tell the teacher. But later in the dorm, as I was getting ready for class, Victoria's boyfriend, Bertie, who was British and strong, attacked me. He beat me like a rabid bull. He was angry at me and told me what I'd said to Victoria. When I met later in the day with Mrs. Scully, she told me to just leave the incident alone because Victoria was "not an angel." But I was afraid Bertie would beat me up again.

> After three years of Eagle Hill and its clear structure and excellent education, we felt somewhat confident we had placed Sammy in a worthy school. As the Maplebrook experience imploded around Sammy, Jane and I were focused on what Sammy could do to solve the problems. He was a fifteen-year-old boy with learning issues asked to live away from home with a population of troubled teenagers. Reading his reflections, we now see that the school did not support him, and that process went on far too long. We learned a powerful lesson. Clearly he was afraid to tell us of all the conflict, rightfully concerned that we would blame him and not understand the dreadful circumstances he was navigating. The institution is not always right. Yes, Sammy made mistakes, but the school leaders failed our son. Unfortunately, the physical fighting and altercations distracted me from the larger issue of the flawed school environment.
> **—Dad, Sam Flood, and Mom, Jane Flood**

Later that night, I tried to apologize to Victoria for what happened at breakfast, but she refused to accept my apology. I yelled at her until Rodrigo, who lived in my dorm, attacked me. I tried to get away from him and kept trying to apologize to Victoria. Rodrigo continued pushing me until I threw at Victoria a book I had in my hand.

As Victoria began to cry, I was still apologizing, but Rodrigo, along with another student, grabbed and tackled me.

After we were separated, Bertie came into my room and screamed at me about what I had done wrong. In retaliation, he threw a book at me and said, "So you like to throw books at girls?" He charged at me. I grabbed his hands, but he ended up clawing my left eye and left a scratch that remained for the entire Winter Holiday break.

The morning after the incident with Victoria, I entered the dining hall and noticed that the students had stopped talking and began eying me angrily. It seemed like all of the students had heard it, and I felt not only publicly humiliated, but also publicly despised. The students never forgot the incident with me and Victoria. They would bring it up in an insulting way even as I tried to move forward. I don't know why they cared so much about Victoria, always coming to her defense and treating me badly. But Maplebrook is a small school, and some of the student bonds were very strong.

Victoria's British boyfriend, Bertie, came from a rich family that lived in New York City. But like the rest of the students at Maplebrook, he was quick to violent tendencies and had anger management problems. Whenever I made him angry talking about Victoria saying the wrong things at the wrong time, Bertie would beat the living daylights out of me.

Sometimes, some of the students would convince Bertie to beat me up for no reason. He would proclaim, "I am King, and you will obey me, subjects."

And I thought, *What subjects? You mean the students in this cramped school?* I told him that he was not a king, but he kept on beating me up. Even after I hit Victoria with a book, he said, "You dare hit the monarch of the realm?"

And I responded: "What realm? You mean this small school? Seems like a very small kingdom with just a baseball field, a soccer field, cafeteria, and a church. Or maybe it's just your delusions of grandeur."

Looking back, I see that Bertie was just another student whom society turned its back on because of his learning disabilities, which made him so quick to anger and threats. Maplebrook didn't seem to help him with those problems; the school just ignored them. One time, I accidently bumped into Bertie when I was walking to the library to do homework, and in response he cussed at me and elbowed me. Whenever I brought up the whole Victoria incident, or other people brought it up, Bertie would get angry and take out all of his frustration on me. I felt bad for him in the end because after I left, Bertie's mom died of cancer a few years later.

Provoked Eagle: Winter of 2010

A girl named Lauren, who spoke with a lisp and acted unfriendly toward me, called me every name she could think of for the word *freak*. One time when I was hugging a student who needed comforting, Lauren said, "Eww." She treated me like a slave when I was clearing the dishes after dinner. I would call her a horrible name. One time, Lauren had some of her friends lock me out of the gym after lunch. But when I was forcing my way into the gym, she kept saying, "Keep the doors locked. I do not want to let this freak in."

I couldn't take the way Lauren was treating me anymore. One day I got into a fight with some students, and Lauren was one of them. I turned my attention to her, grabbed her by her ponytail, and clawed her eye. When she ran to the school nurse, I yelled, "She deserved it."

My mom was very upset with me. I tried to tell her my side of the story, but she told me that two wrongs don't make a right and that she won't let me play video games when I get home. She said the games were the reason I gouged Lauren's eye. I tried to tell her that Lauren was being cruel to me and that most of the students were picking fights with me. Those were the real reasons I clawed Lauren's eye like a provoked eagle.

Devil Worshiper: Spring 2010

Another female student, also named Lauren, who had blonde curly hair and zits all over her face, called me a devil worshiper. One morning while we were having breakfast, I was commenting on how a student named Stephanie tended to cry a lot. I found it kind of funny that she cried over the most mundane things.

Lauren number two overheard me talking and said, "Are you a devil worshiper?"

I was puzzled by what she said.

"A guy who laughs at the misfortune of others, that's what a devil worshiper is." Lauren then went on about the whole Victoria incident. I tried to explain about Victoria not accepting my side of the story and my apology.

But Lauren said, "People don't forgive easily. You know that after you hit her, Victoria was sobbing and said she never wants to come to this school again."

Since the moment Sammy joined our family, we became complete, bonded in a way that most people wouldn't understand. But when I got middle school, I realized that, sadly, other kids weren't quite as accepting as they were just a few years earlier. I became a protective big sister. Not as tough as Mom or as quietly terrifying as Dad, but

> I could hold my own against the pathetic little snots who wanted to feel superior.
> **—Sister, Eliza Flood**

I felt that whenever Lauren and I talked to each other, she was always angry or in a bad mood. But later I found out that she had always loathed me because I told her once that God doesn't exist, and she was extremely religious. I partly believe that I should have known better, but I also thought that was a petty reason to hate someone. The incident that had happened between us was a long time before, and I thought she would have moved on from it. But I got back at her by cutting her down her religion, which is a form of insulting someone. What I'd said was, "You'll be sleeping with the sharks." The sleeping bit was a line I had heard from *The Godfather.* I also said, "You think God is going to give a **** about you?" But she misheard me and told me that I had said she'd be "swimming with the sharks not swimming with the fishes, because I'm a Christian." The insult felt like sweet payback for Lauren calling me a devil worshiper and bringing up the Victoria incident.

Not-So-Hot Time at the Mall

When one of the Maplebrook teachers drove a group of students to a nearby mall, I told her I was going to Hot Topic, a clothing store. When I got back to the group, Lauren was angry at me because the teacher thought I had left the group. I tried to explain to her that I had told the teacher where I was going, but Lauren didn't believe me. "She didn't hear you," she said.

"Yes, she did," I yelled back at her. And by mistake I spat on her because of the retainers I was wearing. She's just one of those people who think that the entire planet revolves around them, and they only care about their image. She'd always bring up how I cut her down and asked me how it made the other Christian celebrities feel when they heard that a girl like Lauren was cut down by a guy like me.

Problems with Other Students

Ester, the girl who was friendly with Victoria, was hostile to me, too, and she gave me angry glares or often called me a freak. I didn't understand why Ester would treat me so poorly until I realized that even though I was being harassed by some other students, I had interrupted her one morning early in the fall while she was eating breakfast. She could have just ignored me! Ester was in the wrong for being petty toward me. From that point on, whenever I tried to be social with her, Ester always said, "You are not my friend."

One time on a winter Sunday afternoon, I got into a fight with a student named Armin, who looked like he had been hitting the gym with his muscular physique. The fight started when I asked another student, Adam, about some holiday background on his computer. He told me to shut up. Armin, who was standing next to Adam, butted in and also told me to shut up. When I screamed an expletive-filled sentence at him, he got offended. I pushed him, he fought back, and a crowd gathered around as we scuffled. A math teacher on dorm duty broke up the fight, and I was sent to my room.

Looking back, we reflect on the moments when we as parents could have and should have seen the issues. Academically, every class we sat through on parents weekend fell well below Sammy's level. Every class was a step backward; he was learning nothing new. With no academic challenges his social growth was affected in a negative way. He wanted to make friends but clearly the students were at different levels, and Sammy was never able to connect.

—Dad, Sam Flood, and Mom, Jane Flood

Later that same day, Armin entered my room with some other students, tackled me, and when I fell to the floor, he tried to strangle me. The same math teacher stopped the fight in time. Worst of all, these students were cheering as Armin strangled me; they seemed to think I deserved to die for something I had not done to them. I felt that the whole incident between me and Armin was unnecessary. He was acting irrational when I was trying to ask another student about something on his computer.

When I first met him, Zach, a student who was as tall as me, was my friend. But after the Lauren eye-gouging incident, Zach became one of my many bullies and for no obvious reason. He would beat me up, either at the gym or at the dining room, slurring stuff like, "Shut up, Sammy" or "You suck." He, like most of the students, would bring up past incidents when I got into trouble.

I couldn't take any more of Zach's bullying, so one day I slammed his eye onto a couch near the bathroom in the dining hall. This incident started as he walked by me and said, "Shut up, Sam," when I had not said anything to him. I got up, grabbed him by the head and shoulder, and slammed his eye on the couch.

He ran into the bathroom.

When I followed him, I saw him fake vomiting near a toilet. I knew he was faking because I saw nothing coming out of his mouth.

Zach turned around to look at me and said, "I'm sick of you!"

Julia, another one of my classmates, was also rude and cruel to me. She was always judgmental whenever I made one small mistake. One time, I got into a fight in the dining room when John, a kid at the table, told me to stop staring at him. "Hey, you better get used to it, or I'll cut your tongue out and shove it up your ***," I snapped back at him. Ash, another student who is as big as I am, tried to calm me down, but I had had enough of how the students had been treating me. Ash grabbed John's arm, but he still managed to punch me in the eye.

After that incident, Julia and another student talked behind my back about what I had done. Later, she told me at a school dance that I "would be the last guy any girl would want to dance with." At the time, I was trying to help out a female student who didn't have a date. Julia used to claim that whenever I sat with her and her friends, I'd always start problems. I did not agree. One time, she told a friend of hers to sit in my seat in the dining room. "You should be more careful where you sit," he said as I tried to get him out of my seat. A teacher told me to stop even though I tried to explain to her that he was in my seat.

One morning when I was going to breakfast, I had just walked up the stairs when a student named Taj grabbed my right arm and tried to drag me back down. He kept on saying loudly for others to hear: "Sam's been cutting in front of everyone in the dorm for years. This is why you don't have any friends. Get the teacher. This needs to end now."

I was just trying to free myself from him. But when the teacher, Mr. Creep, the same teacher who kept one of the students from strangling me, separated us, he blamed me for the whole thing even though Taj could have broken my arm. I thought the teacher downplayed the incident. I also knew that I was at fault for not being aware of my surroundings as I cut in front of everyone before breakfast. Another sign of me being in my own little world.

But Taj should have known that no matter what a person does, he shouldn't respond with violence.

After several months of being picked on by all of these students and by some teachers, I realized that Maplebrook was not the school for me. These students had a lot of problems, and they tended to take them out on me. Some were violent, self-absorbed, uncaring, unlikeable, and mean-spirited bullies. They were wrong when they chose to pick on a big and smart guy like me.

The Worst Roommate I Ever Had

Just like Eagle Hill, Maplebrook had a dorm system where we were paired with a roommate. My roommate was Jade. We had a neutral understanding of each other during the fall of 2009. But after the Lauren eye-clawing incident of midwinter 2010, Jade and I started to mistrust one another. Jade and I barely spoke to each other while we were in our rooms, and sometimes he'd side against me when I got into trouble, mainly because he was with the unfriendly crowd.

Jade was like me in a bad way. For starters, he tended to talk to himself, just as I did and still do sometimes. But Jade rambled like a madman, saying, "Fight the power" and other nonsense. When I talked to myself, it was a way of preparing myself to say something to someone or just repeating what had been said on TV, in a video game, or on the internet. I tried to keep it to myself.

At one point, Jade decided to move into the room next door so he didn't have to listen to me talk to myself. I said I was no different from him, who talked to himself like a maniac. Plus, the room next door had only two beds for the guys living there, and that meant Jade would be sleeping on the floor, which was against dorm regulations. So Jade stayed.

Thieves for a Junkie Teacher

One upsetting fiasco that arose in the late winter was an outbreak of stealing. A thief, or a couple of thieves, would sneak into students' dorm rooms and steal items such as money, watches, headphones, iPads, iPods, books, jewelry, and even one PlayStation Portable. Just like many of the students whose belongings disappeared from their rooms, I was a victim. Not only was my money stolen, but they also took a pair of headphones my dad had given me. I told the dorm teacher, Mr. Don, about the missing headphones, but he didn't do anything. He said I should have written my name on them. But I had just gotten them, and they were stolen two days later. Somehow it was my fault that the headphones were stolen, not exactly great leadership by the teacher. In terms of role models, the school was lacking. The right response should have been, "Let's figure out where they went and solve the problem." Since the teacher wouldn't help, I decided to become a detective and try to break the case of the stolen headphones. I started to ask some of the students who stole my headphones, and they said it wasn't them.

After I left Maplebrook, I found out that the people most responsible for stealing students' belongings were a teacher named Craig and three boys from Bermuda—Josh, Taj, and Jerome. I should have known that the three boys from Bermuda were partly behind the thefts because Josh and Jerome would scam me for their snacks by having me pay for them. I don't know why I kept falling for the same stupid trick. Maybe it's because the three seemed so trustworthy, or I was under the impression they were willing to share with me. But I should have known that they were shady in some way, and I shouldn't have trusted them. Sometimes they would steal my wallet, but I was always able to get it back. It would start when the three boys would enter my room, walk to the bureau, and take my wallet. I would chase after them, but they would disappear. I tried looking around the dorm until I stumbled into one of their rooms and got my wallet back.

My parents heard that the thieves were caught when a foreign exchange student told the teachers that his expensive gold watch had disappeared. The teachers finally decided to launch an investigation. They looked around the entire dorm and finally, they entered Craig's room. Craig was the dorm teacher. They discovered a pile of stolen items and questioned him. He said that he'd persuaded Josh, Jerome, and Taj to steal valuable things while students were either asleep or out of their rooms so he could sell them to a local drug dealer in exchange for coke. This resulted in Craig being fired and Josh, Jerome, and Taj being expelled from school and sent back to Bermuda.

I had not expected that Craig was behind it. I thought he and I had some sort of close friendship; he seemed like one of those cool guys you wanted to hang out with. But there was one incident near Easter 2010, when my family and I went to a fancy restaurant for a nice lunch and stumbled into Craig and his family.

I introduced Craig to my family, and he decided to get too close to my sister's personal space, like he was hitting on her, and he was making creepy remarks about her good looks. My parents noticed that his behavior was a bit odd. I should remind you that Craig was somewhere in his mid or late twenties, and Eliza was eighteen years old.

Part of me knew that he was not the great guy everybody thought he was. I also should have known something was wrong with him when he seemed a bit coked out on most weekends, twitching and acting paranoid. Most of the students didn't really like him because he would take away their personal belongings and never give them back. He was feeding his coke addiction.

Some of the students also felt that Craig acted like a creep with them, and seeing how Craig hit on my sister, I believed them.

I was glad that Craig was fired and that Josh, Taj, and Jerome were expelled and sent back to Bermuda for taking part in all the stealing. I just wish that I had been there to see the looks on their faces when they got kicked out of school and sent home. But I was in a better school, Craig High, at the time that happened, and I did not have to worry about them anymore.

Using my Own World as a Shell: Summer of 2010

Because of the way the school treated me, I began to go onto the internet more often, mainly to watch YouTube videos of *World of Warcraft* as well as other roleplaying games. I spent the entire summer of 2010 on my laptop and acted antisocial, mainly because of how the students at Maplebrook had treated me. By the end of the summer, Dr. Helper told me that I should be on the internet and other forms of media for only one hour a day. I didn't approve, but later he told me that to make more friends, I needed to talk more about other things than just video games, TV shows, and movies. I thought Dr. Helper was wrong, and he was being mean to me by not understanding my likes and also not understanding how much I had suffered from that year at Maplebrook. My parents were trying to get me out of my interest in computer-related activities and to be more social. I believed that my computer refuge was the best way to help me relieve the stress of dealing with selfish, irrational, and unlikeable people like the ones from Maplebrook.

One night at the Ridgewood Country Club, I was discussing my holiday wishlist, and my mom mockingly said, "Video games are a habit."

I angrily pointed my fork at her and snapped back, "Video games are *not* a habit."

My parents did not like that I pointed a fork at my mom. Little did my parents know that the fork-pointing stunt was something students at Maplebrook usually did to me whenever I "offended them."

We visited Dr. Helper again, and he told me that he was trying to help me be more social with people and talk about more than just movies, TV, and video games. I still did not like that I had an only-one-hour media rule. But that feeling didn't last. When I finally graduated from high school three years later in 2013, Dr. Helper lifted the one-hour rule about playing games, being on the internet, and watching TV. He said if I was going to college, I would have a lot of free time on my hands.

I talked about video games and TV shows like an obsessive nerd. I would talk on and on about the certain aspects of what occurred in a show, movie, or video game to the point that people got annoyed. Sometimes they felt uncomfortable with what I was talking about.

Dr. Helper said that if I watched media less, I would be able to find fun things to talk about as a way of expanding my horizons. When I was at Eagle Hill, the school sent letters telling my parents that the students and teachers were a bit uncomfortable with me talking about movies and TV shows all the time. While it was fine to express my interests, there should be a time and place. It is always good to watch your audience, during a conversation, to make sure they are listening to you.

Even though I learned little at Maplebrook, I did learn that some people can be jerks, and I should not hang out with them. I also learned that I wanted to be in a school that challenged me academically, and I didn't want to be warehoused with people who didn't see my academic mind and my social skills. I felt if I had done a better job presenting myself when I interviewed at other potential schools, I would have ended up in a different school with a better education program. And seeing how I was bigger and tougher than everyone, the teachers should have told me not to fight back and just use my head. And I did that, once, by head-butting one of the students who was giving me trouble. And seeing how I felt smarter than some of the teachers, I saw it as a sign that said, "Maplebrook is not the right school for me."

Leaving Maplebrook for Good: Summer 2010

My parents decided to pull me out of Maplebrook because they found out that the school had no college plan for me. I felt that they could have pulled me out of the school sooner instead of waiting for the end of the first week of June. But my dad always says, "Floods finish strong." I should have told him that I wanted to leave the school early because I'd suffered enough with how the students treated me.

> There are no days off with children who learn differently. There is no time to ease up on the process. The job of a parent is 24/7/365, and every day, new challenges emerge. With my constant travel for work, Jane carried most of the burden. Her strength in standing up to the leadership of Maplebrook and calling out the issues rampant at the school, such as having two sets of rules for the students, was amazing. Once we understood that Sammy needed a change, Jane went to work finding the next opportunity.
> —Dad, Sam Flood

Let me end this chapter by telling you again that I did not have a great experience at Maplebrook. The academic program was not challenging and was dumbed down to make it "easier for the students." And although some of the things that happened were my fault, the way students treated me was wrong, even cruel at times.

I thought that Maplebrook was going to help me make some new friends and get a better education, but instead, people treated me poorly, and too many students in that godforsaken school were unkind and mean spirited.

LIFE LESSONS

Sometimes it's best to just walk away.

Don't use your hands, use your head.

It's good to look at your audience when you are in a conversation to make sure they are listening to you.

Chapter 5:

High School Years from Seventeen to Nineteen

(2011–2013)

A Fresh Start

After my parents took me out of Maplebrook, they sent me to The Craig School in Lincoln Park, New Jersey, a forty-minute drive from Ridgewood. At Craig, I got a fresh start in my education. I did well in subjects like literature, writing, history, and science, but I struggled a bit in math, mainly because the concept of graphs and percentages was a bit difficult for me to understand. I eventually got the hang of it.

During the summer of 2010, my parents sent me to the Craig Summer School Program for two reasons. Reason one was to get me acquainted with the school. Reason two was that Maplebrook had failed to give me enough of a challenge. My parents said that summer school would help get my brain working again with tests and homework assignments worthy of my level. Finally, I felt I was actually doing something valuable in the summer school program. Sure, summer school can be a drag for kids and teenagers like me, having to give up their vacation to do a little academic work, but for a student who just got out of a bad school, I felt it was worthwhile for my summer in 2010.

Academic Classes Better than Maplebrook

Craig's academic program provided a challenge I had not had in a long time. I found myself in classes worthy of my grade and age.

Once school started at 9 A.M., I headed to Mrs. Chin's class for math. At first, it was tough because of the graphs and fractions. During my first few weeks, I flunked every test, getting scores of fifty or sixty out of one hundred. One time, I tried to cheat during a math test by using my study sheet, but Mrs. Chin caught me in the act. She talked to my dad about it, and I swore never to cheat again and to study extra hard in math. After that little incident, I got a bit better in math by completing assignments correctly and finishing tests with positive scores.

At 10 A.M., I made my way to biology class, taught by Mrs. Bhakta. The lessons were about plants and photosynthesis. I was fascinated by how plants are able to absorb sunlight as a way of feeding themselves and sometimes grow like human beings. I also learned the various organs within a cell, which fascinated me. There was so much more to learn about biology than what Maplebrook had taught about the human organs.

At 11 A.M., I went to Mr. Jacobs' class for American history. We learned how the colonists arrived and which tribes were in which parts of the country. On some Thursdays and Fridays, Mr. Jacobs had us watch American history movies on certain events such as the Revolutionary War, the founding of America, the Civil War and World War II.

For one assignment, Mr. Jacobs asked us to write a paper on how each X-Men character from the *X-Men* comics would be involved in a historic event in U. S. history. Apparently, Mr. Jacobs was a bit baffled by how the X-Men were involved in the Cuban Missile Crisis in the movie *X-Men First Class*. I chose to write how Magneto, a mutant who has the ability to control metal, was able to stop the assassination of President John F. Kennedy.

Mr. Jacobs skipped most of the *Pearl Harbor* movie whenever we watched it during our World War II lessons. He said, "I did not like the love triangle of the movie." The love triangle involved two pilots who fought over the affection of a nurse. I wished I could have shown him the Nostalgia Critic Review of *Pearl Harbor* during class. The Nostalgia Critic is an internet reviewer who comments on a lot of bad movies. His review was directed at the director Michael Bay's poor attempt in portraying the people who lost their lives during the Pearl Harbor incident leading America to join World War II.

After lunch, I moved on to art with Mrs. Toonkel. I had the most fun in art class because I was allowed to let my creativity run free. I drew pictures of maps of fantasy stories I had come up with, though they tended to look sloppy at times. She taught me how to trace and smoothly draw on the paper, which to me felt relaxing and fun.

Craig School's agenda was to give students the full high school experience. The leadership pushed academics as well as the full array of after-school opportunities. They expected the students to play a sport, join clubs, volunteer in the community, go to prom, and learn to drive cars. They challenged the students to learn public speaking, to build projects for the science fair, and to go to college. They took the time to help a community of students who learned differently and made individual accommodations while holding each teenager accountable.

We were fortunate to watch Sam's confidence grow at Craig. His first semester math struggles were a direct result of a year without challenge or academic expectations at Maplebrook. Once Sam's school brain kicked into gear again, he was back to learning and growing as a student. We remember him learning and reciting full soliloquies from Hamlet. This school made him believe in himself again. Ultimately the doubt that creeps in for kids who learn differently can be debilitating. Craig expected every student to succeed and helped build their confidence.

—Dad, Sam Flood, and Mom, Jane Flood

One day, a problem occurred between me and Mrs. Toonkel. While she was in the bathroom, my friend Tom dared me to lock her out of the classroom. I agreed and locked the door.

When Mrs. Toonkel came back from the bathroom and found the door locked, she started knocking, and the students started laughing.

I finally let her in and backed away.

She asked, "Who tried to lock me out?"

The students told her that I did it.

I tried to tell her that Tom told me to do it, but he denied all allegations. Maybe it's not wise to listen to someone like Tom, who is willing to start trouble just for laughs.

Later in the day, I went to literature class with Mrs. Rubolotta. She taught some of the classic works by William Shakespeare such as *Macbeth* and *Hamlet*. In fact, she usually had us read most of the play that she had rewritten in common language as a way of translating it for the audience who might not understand the

Shakespeare dialogue. We also read from classic works such as *The Crucible* and *The Odyssey*.

I helped Mrs. Rubolotta one Saturday in the fall of 2012, doing a little community service. She and I met with a bunch of teenagers from another school, and we planted some flowers for a garden at a mansion on a wooded hill near the highway that divides Ridgewood and Lincoln Park. Mrs. Rubolotta told me that the mansion was once owned by a rich man from New Jersey who helped fund the Revolutionary War. It was fun to learn a little bit about the surrounding area of Lincoln Park.

For the last period, I headed to the class before study hall, science, with Mr. Simpson. He taught us about the magnetic field, chemistry, the elements, and gravity. Every year I was at the high school, Mr. Simpson came up with some sort of project in the spring to present to the science fair. One year, I was having difficulty coming up with an interesting topic. Mom suggested that I do the "egg drop" experiment, because it related to gravity. I created a rocket ship using cardboard, straw, and other insulation so the egg would be snug, and added decorations. I practiced dropping the rocket ship from the nearest window to see if it landed safely without breaking the egg. After a few trial-and-error tests, I was ready to present my Egg Ship to the science fair. Even though I didn't win the prize, they did like that I put in the effort to present something unique since most of the students had never thought of an egg drop experiment.

Extra Activities

Just like at my previous private schools, I was required to do some extra activities like sports or community service. At Craig High, I ran cross-country in the fall and played basketball in the winter and baseball in the spring.

For cross-country, a few of us would gather outside the school after study hall every Tuesday and Thursday. First, we did a little stretching in order to get prepared for our daily exercises. Then we would jog around the school to start practice. Sometimes, the cross-country coach, Mrs. Chitticks, had us do some drills, which consisted of running up and down a hill on a bridge over nearby train tracks running around the neighborhood behind the school and running back and forth in the parking lot. Like Eagle Hill, Craig High's cross-country team would participate in Morris County, mostly on Saturdays and Sundays. From my point of view, I think it's great that a sporting event should be held on weekends because it gives athletes like me something to do.

At the end of the fall, there was a big race where a couple hundred cross-country runners from different parts of New Jersey gathered around Lincoln Park and ran around the town. During the Cross Country Finals of 2011, I went up to one of the race officials to get our name tags before we started the race.

An older woman asked, "What is your name?"

I replied, "Sam Flood."

She didn't quite hear me, so she asked again.

I snapped and screamed, "MY NAME IS SAM FLOOD!"

My parents witnessed the whole incident and were very disappointed in me. After the race, my parents scolded me for snapping at that old lady even though I tried to explain my side of the story that she wasn't listening to me. They told me that I should be a little clearer and maintain eye contact in order for people to understand me.

During the winter, I started on the Craig High basketball team, and just like at Eagle Hill, I was the star player of the team. After study hall every Tuesday and Thursday, my team and I would go to the town gym for practice. Our coach, Mr. Argenti, would have us do drills like running sprints on the court, practice shooting the ball, and trying to score three pointers. We had some games during the winter session, but most of them took place in the gym at Lincoln Park. Since I was the tallest member of my team, I would be the one to score the most points so we would win, just like we did at Eagle Hill.

Every spring, baseball season would start, and I signed up for it seeing how I was good at baseball at Eagle Hill. Mr Argenti was our baseball coach, too. We usually had baseball practice at a nearby park. We'd do a few practice throws, run around the baseball diamond a few times, practice hitting the ball, and then do a little side tossing and throwing. We also participated in some games just like we did in my Eagle Hill days. I was one of the outfielders who'd sometimes just stand there staring off into space. But whenever a ball was thrown or hit toward my position, I would always run to catch it.

Before school ended for the day, the teachers had students do community service, such as taking out the trash and recycling the papers and cans. During my first year, I didn't do a lot of community service because I was just focusing on my homework. But the principal of Craig High, Dr. Cap, told me that if I didn't do community service, I couldn't graduate. I thought that to be true, so I did some community service whenever the time was convenient to fill the 100-hour requirement.

My mom told me that the Craig School was willing to let anyone graduate, but Dr. Cap wanted to motivate the students to give back to the community.

I was one of those people who helped out my community during the aftermath of a devastating storm in the fall of 2012. When Hurricane Sandy struck the East Coast, Ridgewood was only slightly damaged, but the electricity was another thing. Most of the houses in town, except for ours, lost power, and it took four days for it to be fully restored. Many townsfolk took refuge in the Mount Carmel Church in Ridgewood. Uncle Terry and Aunt Kathryn had to stay on the third floor of our house because their hometown, Franklin Lakes, lost power. My mom thought she could help out the town by giving them a big pot of meatballs in the basement of the church in Ridgewood. I helped out in delivering the meatballs to the church as well as helping Mom in the kitchen. And since the aftermath of the hurricane lasted for about a week, when school reopened, I had filled more than one hundred hours on the school community service list.

My New Best Friends

I made some new friends at Craig, mainly kids in my grade, which was the class of 2013. One of my new friends was Alec, whom I met in class during my first day at school. Alec put together an anime club where we watched such shows as *Soul Eater*, *FullMetal Alchemist: Brotherhood*, *Gurren Lagann*, *Code Geass*, and *Miyazaki* films. I had an interest in anime in a new way, through story-driven episodes, great animation, and well-developed characters.

Nick was another friend of mine who went to many of the same classes as me. He was good at playing cards and sports. After school, Nick, along with a few friends and me, would go to play billiards in a pizza place near town. I had a lot of fun there as we sometimes played arcade games like *Marvel vs Capcom* and *Big Buck Hunter*.

Will, another friend of mine, who had a limp on his left side because he had had a stroke when he was young, was very accepting of his limitations mainly because he had to deal with them all his life. And even though Craig High was willing to help him out, Will also found a way to overcome his limitations on his own. We hung out on a few occasions, like the time my dad took us to a suite to watch a hockey game in the winter of 2011. Alec ended up going to Mitchell College with me. But we hung out with each other less at Mitchell because I was more focused on studying and completing assignments, and he was hanging out with his new friends.

Gabriel and Charlie were identical twins who stood out from the other students. Gabe was the smart one, and Charlie was the funny one. One time Alec, Gabriel, Charlie, Drew, Will, and I all went to a Weird Al concert. We first arrived at Gabriel and Charlie's home, and I was impressed with the log cabin-esque design of their house. We were at Gabe and Charlie's house when we watched *Princess Monoke*, the movie, and I was impressed with the Japanese culture. We went to Hawthorne, which is a twenty-minute drive from Lincoln Park where the concert was being held, and I felt that I could have gone to the city more often and just hung out there.

Cameran, a fellow classmate from U. S. history, was a lot like me, tall, funny, and athletic. Today, he works at one of my town's restaurants, which is called The Office. He and I bump into each other whenever my family and I go there, and we chat about what we've been up to.

My friends and I did get into small conflicts at times. One time during lunch in 2013, we were discussing our trip to a water park, where some employee acted completely stupid when she forgot to take our order. I said, "We oughta smack her upside her head," a line I had learned from my mom whenever she jokingly threatened me.

Ben, a fellow classmate of mine replied, "Maybe you should write a joke in your graduation speech."

I thought he was mocking me, so I said back at him, "Maybe you should write a suicide note."

Suddenly, Matt, a short guy, was offended. He stood and said, "My friend wrote a suicide note, and he killed himself." Matt was in tears as he stormed out of the dining room.

Mrs. Sloan, who was the student counselor, asked me to come over to her office, and she told me about how I hurt Matt's feelings by telling that suicide joke.

I told her the full story and how Ben suggested I write a joke during my graduation speech. I thought he was making fun of me, and I told him to write that suicide note.

My mom got word of the whole thing, and she swore never to say, "I'll smack you upside your head" again.

What I've learned from that incident is that maybe it's not a good idea to make jokes about suicide because it is a very serious subject.

My friends and I had similar interests, such as video games, comics and anime. I felt like the kids in the class of 2013 were the only real friends I had in the school. Craig High was the only high school where people treated me like a person and not a whipping boy. I couldn't relate to the students at Maplebrook because of how unlikeable they were. At Craig, the students did not go out of their way to pick fights with other students or find new ways to harass students like me. Sure, we did get into a little bit of a conflict once in a while, but a teacher usually found neutral ground for us to both agree that we were right and we were wrong. And seeing how most of the students in my class are males, it meant we were a big gang that had a close bond.

Becoming a Writer

I began to develop a high interest in role playing games (RPG) during my 10th grade year. This involved dressing up as a certain character and going around the world killing monsters to level up, mainly through the *Dragon Age* series as well as the *Elder Scroll* series through the PlayStation 3. I began to view the world as a fantasy RPG with elves, dwarves, qunari (a race of horned giants), humanoids with fox ears and a tail, orcs, gnomes, and lizard people. *Dragon Age* taught me to think things through before going full ahead with my decisions, and it helped me become the adult I am now.

My mom and I would watch *Game of Thrones* every Sunday night in its premiere season in 2011. Funny story. When my parents and I were watching season three of *Game of Thrones*, we saw the infamous "Red Wedding" episode. My mom was horrified that Rob Stark, the King of the North; Talia Stark, the Queen of the North; and Caitlyn Stark, Rob's mother (as well as Grey Wind, Rob's pet wolf), were killed off at the wedding.

I told them to shush because I had read the book series that Game of Thrones was based on, *A Song of Ice and Fire*, so I know all about the Red Wedding, an event that took place in the third installment of the book series called *Storm of Swords*.

Learning How to Drive

I started to learn how to drive in 2011, when I was in tenth grade. After I got my permit, I practiced driving with my parents on a regular basis. When I first started driving in the summer of 2011, I was afraid I might crash, but over time, I got the hang of it, like riding a bike. I was good at parking, turning, stopping, and going with the flow of traffic, but I had trouble parallel parking because it was difficult turning my head one way and another while I was focusing so hard. In the fall of 2011, after I did a little student driving with a driving instructor from the DMV in Wayne, which is near Craig, he decided not to give me a driver's test appointment because he felt I wasn't ready, mainly because I needed to parallel park better.

I think that the DMV felt I was not ready because of my learning disabilities. Some of the students say that the Wayne DMV was terrible because they treated most of their students unpleasantly and unfairly. Alec told me that the DMV failed him so many times after he made only one simple mistake on the driving test. I tried to take the driver's test in 2013, but I was told that my written test had expired, and I had to take it again on the computer. I tried but failed because the computerized written test was too difficult for me. All of the questions were timed, and I didn't have time to think things through. So I rushed ahead and got the wrong answer. I would have done the written test again after I graduated from high school, but I realized that I had to focus on graduating from college and then find a way to complete the written test in the future.

My dad sometimes mocks me for not having a driver's license. He says that even though I don't need to drive, it is good to have a license in case I need to drive. While that's his way of stimulating me to get back onto my "driving" feet, I've always felt weak in the eyes of most people my age who have driver's licenses. So I've decided that sometime this year, I will try again. The reason I am thinking of doing it now, instead of the times I was home during my college days, is that I was just trying to relax after all of the stress I had to go through in college. Even when I started the process to get my driver's license, I was always afraid of getting into a car accident if I was not careful and end up either dead or paralyzed. I would not be able to do the things I used to do, and I would have been a burden my entire life on the people I care about. But that's just me obsessing about things that most likely won't happen. I am much more focused now than I was in the past.

The driving was a fascinating study in the school expecting the students to accomplish the same life milestones as any other teenager. Sammy passed the written permit test and had the slip of paper that allowed him to drive with a parent in the passenger seat. Driving with the big guy was at first a scary prospect, but once he slid his big body behind the wheel, he was really very good. He was calm and focused on the task. He was actually a better driver than his older sister when she was driving with her permit. For Sammy, there was never a misstep, but there was fear. He was afraid of getting in an accident, afraid of getting a ticket, and afraid of the driving test.

We started practicing how Sammy would deal with a police officer if he ever got a ticket. We would walk up to the window of the car and role play giving Sammy a ticket. We would go through what questions he might be asked and how he should respond. It clearly made Sammy very apprehensive about the potential of being alone in the car. We also talked about what would happen if he was involved in a fender bender and how he would deal with another driver. This scenario also gave Sam distress. He hates to disappoint people, and as we role played, he would apologize for the potential incident even if we said the other driver had run a red light and hit Sam's car.

Ultimately, we think Sammy was relieved when he did not have to take the driving test and did not get his license. He is fortunate that Uber and Lyft came around at just the right time for a young adult without a license. That being said, we think one day, he will want the independence of driving a car and being able to hit the road by himself. We know he will be a great driver, and he is now well equipped to deal with a ticket or a fender bender.

—Dad, Sam Flood, and Mom, Jane Flood

First Time in London

During my senior year at Craig High, I traveled to England for the first time. I actually went to England twice, first for Wimbledon and second for the London Olympics. When I first arrived in London, I was a bit disoriented with the different time zones, but I got used to it. During my first day there, a friend of my dad took my mom and me around the city. I've learned so many great things about London, like how some of the architecture was made during the Roman Empire. We visited the various theaters and wondrous sites such as Big Ben, the Tower of London, and London Bridge. I wish I could have gone to Buckingham Palace to see the royal family, but I guess they were pretty busy then.

When I arrived at the hotel where my dad was staying near Wimbledon, he told me to eat dinner even though it was 11:30 at night. But since I didn't have any dinner during my plane ride, and I was still a bit confused by the plane ride, I decided to try out British food. I took a bite out of the steak, and it felt like I was in heaven. The meat tasted so much more flavorful than it is in America. I soon discovered that European food is better than American food because they don't put chemicals into the ingredients that we Americans do to make our dishes.

I finally got to see where my cousins Charlie, Hugh, and Hayley lived in South West London. I was a bit dismayed because I thought my cousins lived in the big city, in an apartment, but instead they lived in one of those British suburbs you see on British TV shows like *Dr. Who* and *Coronation Street*. But then again, the street that they lived on looked nice, and we had some fun together playing *Fable 2* on their XBOX 360.

My mom decided we should go to the amusement park near the town. I thought it would be fun going to a British version of an amusement park. But when my cousins and I got to the place, it wasn't what I expected. The park was broken down, a mediocre place with rides that lasted no more than a minute. They gave prizes that you would throw away in a day or two, sold cheap branded snacks, and offered a Ferris wheel ride that almost killed me because there were no safety railings on the ride. But at least we were able to do something.

During the end of an Olympic basketball match, I told them that I was headed back to the hotel I stayed at because I'd had a long day dealing with all of the noise and flashing lights in the Olympic stadium. So I took the train and rode all the way back to my hotel room, all by myself. Uncle Dick offered to take me back to the hotel, but I told him that I could handle it. That was the first time I was able to go all the way from a part of a big city to the place I was staying at by myself. I know that Uncle Dick was willing to help me because he'd been in London longer than I had, so he knew his way around. But I wanted to prove that I was willing to do things on my own, mainly because I was eighteen during the London Olympics, and I wanted to do things for myself for once. And I did just that, hopping on that train and traveling back to the hotel with no problems.

Finally Getting into College

During the second half of my senior year at high school, I was accepted to Mitchell College in New London, Connecticut. Before the interview, I felt I was going to mess up by yawning and be rejected for admission. But I held it together and did the interview with no screwups.

A month after the interview, while I was at a pizza shop, I got a phone call saying that I got accepted into Mitchell College. It was the happiest day of my life. In my mind, I felt I could hear the song "I've Got a Golden Ticket," a song from *Willy Wonka and the*

Chocolate Factory, playing when I got accepted. My parents were happy because they'd known I would go to college despite what some of the doctors had said about me not being able to qualify because of my learning disability. As it turns out, Mitchell is one of those colleges that helps out people with learning disabilities. I guess going to the right schools, such as Eagle Hill and Craig High, did pay off.

My parents also believed that because Mitchell is a small college, it would make it easy for a guy like me to navigate the area. When my parents and I were dropping off Eliza at Dickinson College, I started to wander around the campus.

A campus security guard saw me and asked me if I was lost.

I told him I wasn't lost, and he went on his way, but my dad saw this and scolded me for getting lost on campus grounds.

I told him that I was just minding my own business by wandering around the area.

Dad told me that Dickinson is a big area, and I could easily get lost, so I needed to go to a small college so I could navigate the area better.

I graduated from Craig High School with flying colors, which made my parents and my family very proud of my accomplishments.

How Craig High Helped Me Succeed

Craig High helped me out the most in maturing into an adult and dealing with my learning disabilities to help me get into college. The school pushed me to become the student I could be. My parents pushed me harder to succeed as well. They believed in me because I was one of the students who can succeed despite my learning differences, and they saw me as a normal person. I believe that my parents made the right call in transferring me to

Craig High because I was able to get into a good college, something that society thought I could never do because of my learning disabilities.

LIFE LESSONS

Always focus in class.

Be thankful for the friends you have.

Never bring anything sensitive to a conversation.

Find inspiration for your creativity.

Schedule your days to get your life right.

Always improve yourself in order to succeed.

Chapter 6:
College Years
(2013–2018)

After I graduated from Craig High School, I spent five years at Mitchell College in New London, Connecticut. I earned a lot from college, both as an adult and as a student. I learned that college is a lot different from high school in that you're learning to live on your own. Seeing how I learned how to live on my own during my Eagle Hill years, it wasn't a challenge. (And I don't usually get homesick.) I also learned that violence doesn't solve everything, and everyone disagrees or disapproves of what you want out of life. These are the stories of those lessons I learned during my years in college.

Thames Academy

I first attended Thames Academy, a one-year boarding academy that is part of the Mitchell College program. Thames teaches students how to function in a college environment with practice classes such as technology and historical arts. They also offer aid to any students struggling in class by guiding them on what to do in future sessions. Private tutors help students with their homework.

My roommate at Thames was Simon; he moved in with me after his previous roommate turned out to be a psychopath who tried to kill him. We got along fine, although some of Simon's friends harassed me at times. One student, Hayden, would stick out his tongue at me and just stand there. This would annoy me a lot, and I would tell him to stop. But he wouldn't listen.

One time, I tried to go to the dorm proctor, but Hayden blocked my path. I tried to get away from him, but he just kept pushing me. Left with no option, I said, "Screw it!" I kicked him in the privates, which was the first time I had ever kicked someone like that.

Hayden fell to his knees and groaned in pain.

My dad told me afterward that hurting someone like that is "unprofessional." This moment resulted in my getting a "no contact" order, which forbade me from ever speaking to Hayden.

Later on, I got into another fight with a friend of Hayden who was also harassing me. This fight also resulted in my getting a "no contact" order, forbidding me from speaking to that student as well.

The dorm security guard told me that if I got into another fight, I would be expelled from college, so I swore to myself that I would never hurt anyone physically again. I learned that violence is never the answer and it could make things worse not just for me but for the people around me. I tried my best to control my anger and never get into fights.

My first few weeks at Thames weren't successful. Even though I knew how to live away from home, I was failing most of the subjects because they were much more advanced than the ones I'd learned at Craig High. I did most of my homework in my dorm room, a place of distraction because I would just goof off, listen to music, or watch YouTube videos.

My parents weren't pleased with me for getting low grades in every class. They told me to get my act together and do my homework in the library. So from that point on, for the rest of my college years, I did all of my work in the library. I was also doing poorly because most of the homework was hard to understand. But my advisor told me that it was okay for me to go to a teacher and learn how to do the assignment correctly. So I did. After classes, I went to a private tutor, and we went over the question and read the textbook to get clearer answers. If I was struggling on an essay, the tutor and I would read over the textbook the essay was based on.

Sammy's trips to the library to study gave him a safe space to stay focused on task number one, which was to earn the degree that didn't seem likely given his original diagnosis. As parents, we were thrilled that he figured out the academic drill, and we were able to see his creative side flourish. He had the ability to write and build storylines that engaged his professors. The graphic design work showed us once again the value of computers to unleash Sammy's creativity. His posters and script-writing work built his confidence. That academic confidence did not solve the friendship dilemma but did give him a sense of success and accomplishment.

—Dad, Sam Flood, and Mom, Jane Flood

Even though I had been reported as a student who had poor grades, I received a reward upon graduating from Thames Academy, for being the most improved student that year. I guess I got better because my parents' criticism made me want to improve by being more focused in my studies and trying my best to improve on getting a better grade on my assignments. I did not want to let them down.

How My Roommate Tried to Kill Me

In 2014, after I completed my Thames year, I began my freshman year at Mitchell College. I lived at Matteson Hall and roomed with Josh, who had shaved his head. The summer before, my parents found out that Josh was going to be my roommate and thought that he and I might be friends. So Josh and I talked on the phone during the summer, and he said that he was looking forward to meeting me. But during the first week of freshman year, Josh ignored me. He would often just go out, and when I returned to our room after doing homework at the library, I'd ask him where he had been. He would not answer me. But when I kept asking him, he told me to "shut it."

One day, I asked Josh about what he had been doing, and again he told me to "shut it." So he and I got into a huge argument, and I said that his mom was a whore and his dad was worthless. A friend of his entered our room and put a stop to it. I thought that would be the end of the disagreement, but it kept going when I told Josh's friend about people who would treat me badly and give me weird looks, mainly this one blonde girl named Stella.

Stella had seen me at the cafeteria during my Thames year and apparently was unimpressed by the "weird" things she saw me doing, such as the way I sat or the way I ate. Because when I first started Mitchell College proper, Stella freaked out when she saw me and said, "Oh no, not him."

When I mentioned Stella, Josh started to act like a jerk, saying that she treated me poorly because she thought I was "a creep." So, Josh and I argued more, and we ended up fist fighting. Josh threw the first punch, and I fought back in self-defense. Things got dangerous when Josh grabbed a box cutter from his desk and tried to slice me, but he didn't succeed. Josh's friend contacted campus security, and the security guard dragged Josh out of our room. Campus security confiscated the box cutter.

The day after the fight, my mom came to Mitchell, and we talked about the whole incident with the head of the dormitory. We were able to piece together that Josh was a threat, and the dorm head said Josh and I shouldn't be roommates anymore. Josh moved out of Matteson, and I stayed in a single room for my four college years. My fight with Josh made me realize that sometimes roommates are not going to be friends, and I should just leave people to their own business.

We take so much for granted in human interaction. We take nonverbal and even verbal cues to understand boundaries and possibilities. Watching Sammy navigate the relationship side of life was both frustrating and eventually very rewarding.

The Maplebrook battles turned into three successful years at Craig High School. We were hopeful that Sammy was aware of how his behavior impacted others. The thought and hope was that the violent confrontations of those Maplebrook years were in the rearview mirror. But as this chapter reveals, there was more growing and learning for Sammy to find his place in society. It's also clear how uncomfortable it can be when people look at you differently and, more importantly, judge you to be different and don't respect you.

Sammy needed to learn how to take cues from his peers and read the room. Clearly our urging to be friends with his roommate was taken literally and had a negative impact on his freshman year.

A phone ringing at 2:35 in the morning is never going to bring good news. So when our phone came to life that early fall morning, we were scared for Sammy. Jane immediately jumped in her car and drove the two hours to Mitchell College to deal with the issue and make sure Sammy would be protected moving forward. One more trip for Jane on 95 North to support Sammy in his complicated journey.

Sammy started by apologizing for having gotten into a fight after promising he was done with physical confrontations. We were disappointed and then suddenly stunned to learn his roommate pulled out the box cutter. That was a real threat and a major issue. We immediately asked Sammy to put security or the dorm leader on the phone. The RA jumped on and said it was a non-issue and had been settled. She also explained that the roommate was moved to another dorm for the night and Sammy was fine.

Sammy might have been physically fine, but emotionally, he was in a rough spot. The failure to make friends with his roommate bothered him more than the box cutter. We started to understand that the pressure to make friends had created an obsession for Sammy. His struggle reading verbal and nonverbal cues was impacting his transition into adulthood. The knife and the drama of that emotional night certainly didn't ease this struggle.

—**Dad, Sam Flood**

Psycho Student

I thought that the Josh fiasco would be the only incident during my freshman year. But I also got into an argument with a girl named Stephanie when she and her friends were debating Chinese takeout. They were talking about Golden Wok and the First Wok in New London. Seeing how I'd tried First Wok, I said that would be the best place to have takeout. I also noticed that there was a First Wok menu on the table in the common area of Mattenson, but there was no Golden Wok menu available.

Stephanie insisted there was a Golden Wok menu, and I got into her face while we argued.

A female student I did not know entered our dorm and broke up the argument. I told her that it was not her place to tell people what to do because she was not a teacher. But she told me that all she wanted was for students to get along with each other, and I owed Stephanie an apology for yelling at her.

Deep down, I know I started the argument by choosing to prove someone wrong about the Chinese takeout menu. Part of me felt I could have walked away from Stephanie when she and her friends were discussing which Chinese restaurant they should try, but I wanted to prove her wrong.

The next day, I tried to apologize to Stephanie, but she raced away from me on her scooter and screamed at me to get away from her. The three students who saw her react that way told me that Stephanie was a little bit crazy and that I should stay away from her.

That afternoon, outside of the cafeteria, before I was about to have dinner early so I could do my homework in the library, I tried to apologize to Stephanie about the argument.

She got angry with me and told me that I got into her face.

I tried to be reasonable, but she said she was going to kick my butt. I told her to go ahead, and she would get herself expelled, but she said her parents owned the school.

This could not be true, I thought. My grandfather Floodo was friends with the dean of Mitchell College, and he said there was no information on Stephanie's parents owning the school. I know that some of Stephanie's friends bought into her lie, but deep down I felt that the reason why Stephanie said her parents owned the school was so she could pretend that people actually liked her because of how important she and her family were in the school.

Sometimes when I talked to Stephanie, I could feel her spitting and cursing at me, always willing to argue with me when I tried to be the sane person.

As the feud between me and Stephanie got out of hand, most of the friends I had made during my freshman year, such as Doug, a kid who lived on my floor, and Danielle, who hung out with me in the gym every Sunday, turned against me. They'd heard I had been harassing Stephanie. One of Stephanie's friends, Tyler, told me that Stephanie had been suffering from mental health issues, dealing with school work, and having family problems back at home.

When I tried to talk things out with Stephanie the day after my initial argument, she was offended and stormed out of the dining hall. Three days later, she filed a "no contact" order against me.

Looking back, I see that the situation was kind of my fault, like the time I told Eliza about Marco dying. I should have kept my mouth shut. But I thought that talking to Stephanie would end our feud. I also learned that maybe sometimes I need to keep my mouth shut to avoid offending people.

Another student, Ben, acted rude and unfriendly toward me. The incident started when I accidently cut in front of some students in the cafeteria, and I wasn't fully aware that I had done so. Ben called me a name. I asked him why he was being cruel toward me, and for some reason, he threatened to call campus security. This was strange when all I did was say "Hi" to him nicely. But he ignored me and acted like I didn't even exist. I tried to ask him again, but he called campus security and filed a "no contact" order on me as well. The strange thing is, I didn't do anything to warrant the no-contact order; I was just trying to be friendly to him, and he acted rude toward me for no reason. It felt like Ben was acting like those jerks back at Maplebrook School, treating me like I was a horrible person when it was the other way around. But back then, I should have respected his wishes to stay away from me, and maybe our history would have been different.

I tried later to talk things out with Danielle, one of the students who turned on me, but she wouldn't have any of it because of the way I had treated her friend Stephanie. When I tried to apologize to her again, she said I did not have to talk to her.

So I said, "Let it go," and called her a terrible name used on women.

She replied by saying she wasn't that and called me a name often used for abusive men. And that was the end of our friendship.

In my defense, I thought she was acting irrationally mainly because she didn't want to hear my side of how the Stephanie feud started. Whenever I tried to explain myself, Danielle would always say, "That's not what she said." I thought that gave me the right to call her what I did.

This feud continued during my time at Thames, and my friend Joey said that it was not okay to call a woman that, even though I explained that the real reason Danielle detested me is because I "bullied and harassed" her friend Stephanie. Those were Danielle's words, not mine. I never harassed or bullied Stephanie at any time. And sometimes, I felt like Danielle was acting immature and rude to me for one simple insult I said to her. I was trying to rekindle our friendship, but she chose to act rude in response to my attempt to apologize. I knew if I hadn't called Danielle that word, our history would have been different.

Another guy, Nick, a student who lived in my dorm, loathed me when he found out about my "harassing" Stephanie and Ben and getting no-contact orders. But he seemed more afraid of me, like I was about to hurt him or something. One time during dinner, Nick donned a fake European accent because apparently he thought I might be impressed. I don't know what he was trying to accomplish with that fake accent. All I know is that it made Nick look foolish. He thought I was the stupid one. Because of my language processing disability, he thought I would not understand a single thing he said. But I wasn't so dumb to fall for his tricks and told him to drop the act. Nick claimed that he was smart because he was a robotic engineer. I thought he was not that smart if he felt that using a fake accent and hiding from me because I "bullied and harassed" his friends made him look intelligent. I knew that he was willing to use my learning disability as some way to get back at me.

After those incidents during my freshman year, I swore to never get too emotional again and just focus on trying to get along with other people. Otherwise, I realized, my only college friends would be the teachers.

> In an effort to build social connections, we met with the college president and asked how the school could help Sammy become part of the Mitchell community. Two great opportunities opened up for Sammy. First, he became a part of the women's basketball team as a manager. That role gave him a dozen young women who knew his name and appreciated that he was there for them helping practice run smoothly. The respect he earned from the players made him feel a part of that hoops community. It was one more step toward belonging and not feeling like an outcast. A great reminder how structure and a nudge opens doors and starts a new chapter in life. It certainly helped that at six feet and seven inches, Sammy could help rebound and collect basketballs for the team.
>
> As for the second opportunity, Sammy started working in the admissions office. He was not ready to lead tours, but he was ready to be part of another community of folks dedicated to recruiting the right student body for Mitchell College. The admissions director was

a chatty fellow who forced Sammy into conversations and gave him tasks that helped him learn how to work in an office. We were thrilled to watch Sammy become part of two organizations that cared about him and included him in their worlds.

These lessons of inclusion and opportunity are wonderful reminders to look out for the quiet or socially awkward person. It is a winning example of creating a purpose and a platform to engage with people. People need people, and folks who learn differently need to have doors thrown open.

—Dad, Sam Flood

Graphic Design and Other Classes

I majored in graphic design at Mitchell. I didn't do so well during my freshman year because the whole experience was new to me, and I didn't have an Apple computer of my own. I just used an HP laptop to do most of my homework, but through my college years, I got better as I did most of my graphic design work in the classroom itself.

My teacher, Mrs. Ward, was very proud of all of the projects I created for her. In fact, there was one class assignment in which the class and I had to come up with drawings and cut them in half to see how they look on other cut pictures. I drew different pictures of elven knights of every kind. The fair-skinned wood elves, high elves, mountain elves, and half elves; the purple-skinned dark elves; the dark-skinned desert elves; the blue-skinned sea elves and snow elves, and the pale-skinned moon elves. We all presented our designs on a Friday.

Mrs. Ward said we could trade around our "half and half" drawings and keep them for the summer. Everyone was impressed by my elven knights; they took all my drawings back home.

I also took classes in history, writing, math, literature, science, and social studies and got A's and B's, mainly B's. I struggled with marine ecology. It was a hard subject, and I couldn't keep up with the material. I started to develop feelings of failure, but with help from a tutor, I was able to complete my marine ecology assignments. I ended up getting a D, which was my worst grade. I learned that marine ecology wasn't the right class for me.

I did great in world history, taught by Mr. O'Leary. I learned a lot about how civilization started in the ancient Middle East and how small city states became the first kingdoms of the world. I was interested in Roman history and how Christianity was the Empire's attempt to keep their empire from crumbling. But I was late on one assignment on the Mississippi during the 1860s. I was caught up with other homework assignments. Plus, I was goofing off during the weekend, and I didn't complete it in time and email it back to O'Leary. Even though I told Mr. O'Leary the truth about how I slacked off, he gave me a C+. But at least he was impressed by the fact that I was honest about my mistake.

I was also able to join the anime club, but that was on the main college campus away from the academy.

Becoming a Writer

I also took a script-writing class and started to develop my talent. During the class, I mainly wrote commercials or parodies of funny commercials such as Skittles and Mountain Dew. We were given a special assignment to create a short story screenplay. During the process, I came up with an idea of four adventurers: a human knight, an elven archer, a dwarven warrior, and a human mage adventuring together to slay an evil demon-worshiping wizard, and I named the story *Fantasy Quest*. The class read it and even though they felt that the screenplay was a bit too long, they enjoyed it. I presented my screenplay to my uncle Terry, and days later, he told me to change the name in order to avoid copyright claims, so I renamed it to *Party of Four Heroes*. I've been a fantasy writer ever since, mainly just writing *Party of Four Heroes 2, 3, 4, 5, 6,* and *7* as well as some spinoffs, using the screenplay style of writing I learned at Mitchell.

I also took some movie study classes where we watched films and wrote reports about the different kinds of techniques such as filming, genre, sound, and story.

In 2017, during my senior year at Mitchell, I was given an assignment to watch *Blade Runner 2049* and write a compare and contrast report about it and the first version released in theaters in 1982. When I realized that the movie theaters in Ridgewood didn't play *Blade Runner 2049*, I found out that the only theater playing the movie was in New York City. So my mom took me to see the movie, and she fell asleep while I wrote notes on it.

Friends in College and My First Crush

I made some friends in college such as Joey, a sports fan who lived in my dorm; Tex, a senior who was into anime and the president of the anime club; Chris, a Goth who was also a member of the anime club; Simon, my roommate during the year at Thames; Luke, my roommate during my senior year; Tyler, another guy who lived in my dorm; Conner, a guy I hung out with in the cafeteria and was the president of the anime club after Tex graduated; and Dan, a fellow classmate of mine who went to a few classes with me including graphic design. Even though I was mostly focused on studying to get good grades, I often hung out with them in the cafeteria and had fun conversations. We also met during college fairs and played games together.

While at Mitchell, I also started developing feelings for some of the female students. One in particular was a woman named Amy. When I first saw Amy during my freshman year, I was blown away by her beautiful looks and funny and friendly personality. I thought about asking her out, but she had a boyfriend, so I just acted like a friend toward her. During my sophomore year, I began to spend more time with Amy, and we learned more about each other. But when I was about to confess my feelings to Amy, I discovered she wasn't at the college anymore. A student told me she had transferred to a medical school. I had myself to blame for not telling Amy my feelings toward her, but I soon learned that sometimes we can't always get what we want. I also learned that I should be respectful toward my friends and their romantic partners. Sometimes in life, some people aren't the right love interest for you, and maybe you should find someone who loves you for who you really are.

> It was frustrating to watch the relationship part of Sammy's life at college. He badly wanted friends and told me he was ready for a college girlfriend. His struggles reading the room made this a bumpy road. We would celebrate the small victories when he would discuss his friend group for lunch or dinner. He was happy to be at the table and perhaps not say much, but he learned to be comfortable with people outside his family. He finally learned it was not right to demand acceptance and not appropriate to be rude or condescending in response to a perceived slight.
>
> —**Dad, Sam Flood**

Senior Year Jobs

During my junior and senior years, I took some internships and jobs at Mitchell. I became assistant manager for the women's basketball team. My role was to set up training exercises for the team, and I gave my support by going to their home games.

I also took part in an internship in graphic design with my teacher Karen. My job was to design posters for college events. I sent my posters to Karen, and she told me to work on multiple versions of the same poster to see which ones worked and which ones didn't.

I took another internship working at the Admissions office at Mitchell College. My main job was reorganizing files and helping the people who worked at the Admissions office to create cards for students who had been accepted. My junior year and senior year were pretty busy as I had less homework and more work at my college jobs, and my parents were preparing me for the work environment after I graduated.

Wisdom Teeth Pain

I had my wisdom teeth extracted in 2016, when I had finished my second year in college. When I was first told that I had to get my wisdom teeth yanked out, the local dentist said that they were going to remove one wisdom tooth per week, but when I got to the special dentist who performed the surgery, he said that I would get all four removed in case one wisdom tooth grew to be impacted.

On the day of my extraction, the dentist injected Novocain in my gums with a needle. I barely remember what happened after they shot my gums because I somehow closed my eyes and when I woke up, my mouth was in pain. Turns out I was knocked out for an hour. I was bleeding through my nose because when the dentist extracted one tooth, it affected my sinuses. I was in severe pain because all four teeth were yanked out. My mom drove me home and had to help me walk all the way to the family room while I was bleeding through my mouth and nose.

She went to get some painkillers at CVS.

I was in so much pain that I texted my mom and said, "I'm bleeding through my mouth and nose. Where the **** are you, you *****?"

She came home and was very upset that I had texted her and called her that horrible name.

In my defense, I was in pain from all that Novocain and the wisdom tooth extraction, so I wasn't thinking. I spent the entire week recovering. It sucked that I had to cut most of my food up because of the stitches in my gums. I ate mostly pasta, chopped up burgers, and milkshakes. Sometimes I'd just swallow the food like a pelican.

My dad thought that if I went to Rhode Island, which I did, swimming in the salt water would help heal my stitches. When I finally got my stitches removed, I felt like I was free from all of the pain in my gums and free from having to eat chopped-up foods.

Fat Shaming the Dog

During Thanksgiving of 2017, the British Floods, the Fritzes, Uncle Larry and Aunt Tyler, and Floodo and Sally were all gathered at Floodo and Sally's house in Rhode Island. I noticed that the Fritzes' dog Crosby had a large gut on him, so I fat shamed him. I said to the dog, "Looks like Crosby is gaining a little bit of a gut. He's small and fat." This caused Crosby to hide from the rest of the family because apparently his feelings were hurt. I thought that it was okay to make fun of a dog or cat, but not okay to physically hurt a dog or cat.

The Fritzes thought that while I was joking around, they also felt that it wasn't nice to make fun of a dog's body image, as dogs have feelings, too. Especially in front of my relatives who own the dog. I basically hurt their feelings as well as Crosby's.

Twenty-First Birthday

During my college years, I turned twenty-one, meaning I could legally drink. And so my family arranged a surprise birthday party at Park West Tavern in Ridgewood. I had my first taste of alcohol, which was cider. I did not like it, so I just ate mini burgers and mini steaks and desserts for most of my twenty-first birthday. It was one of the best days of my life.

My parents told me stories of how they celebrated their twenty-first birthdays, and Eliza told me how she celebrated her twenty-first birthday with her friends. They all told me what kind of drinks they had and how much fun they had with their college friends. I felt like I was the only one in the family who didn't celebrate my twenty-first birthday with my friends, but I had a good time stuffing my face, and I hardly drank at all. I had a fun time.

Speaking of drinking, I never drank alcohol in college mainly because most of the bars were in New London. Also, most of the students mainly smoked pot. I thought that college was a time in most people's lives when they could eat like crap, dress like slobs, make love any time of the week, drink until they got alcohol poisoning, and smoke weed until they get lung cancer years later. Apparently, Mitchell College was the college where many of the students smoked pot for medicinal reasons. Sometimes they couldn't sleep, or they had vision or sinus issues or other health problems that were apparently only solved by smoking pot. I could smell the weed smoke a mile away. I felt back then that I could have smoked pot with some of my peers, but my mom said it could give me lung cancer.

Trips to Sarges

During some of my Saturdays, I would go to Sarges, the New London comic book store, and buy comics or graphic novels, spending like a drunken sailor, as the comics themselves were a bit pricey. I would go to a burger restaurant or pizza place and have lunch. The walks to and from Sarges felt long. I also felt like the more I entered New London territory, the more danger I was putting myself in because the city was a bit broken down and crime ridden in some areas. But once I knew my routine and felt safe, the more I walked around New London. It felt like I was learning how to live in a city. Sure, it's not as big or grand as New York or Boston, but there were some fun sights in New London, such as the water fountain near the train station or the wharf overlooking the Thames River in Connecticut.

My senior year, I went to a burger place to celebrate Saint Patrick's Day. I ordered a bacon burger as well as a Guinness, and I took a taste of it. I thought it was okay, so I posted a picture of it and sent it to my family. I also had a key lime cake, and when I took my first bite of it, I felt a little excitement in my mouth and kept on eating more.

At Mitchell, I created my first resume, where I placed all of my information, including my job and education history. When I attended a program called Broad Futures, Alexa and Carolyn suggested I update it a little bit. I learned that having a resume is important to get a good job. I had planned originally to take a summer internship, but for some reason, that was canned, which was a good thing seeing how the interns would just be living in the college campus area within Washington D. C. during the summer. I did not want to live in Washington D. C. during the summer.

Graduation

During my graduation week, the class and I went to Mohegan Sun, a casino resort in Connecticut, near New London. We all had a blast because we found out that Mohegan Sun was more than just a casino; it was a mall as well. There were so many restaurant options for me to choose from.

Tyler suggested I try the burger place called Social Bar. I tried it and thought it was good, but part of me felt that I should have tried the pizza place. While I did have fun at the burger restaurant, how I spent the night in my hotel room was not fun because my roommate snored the entire night away and woke me around 5 A.M. I talked to my roommate about how his snoring woke me up, and he said that it was just like an episode of *Spongebob*.

On Graduation Day, May 12, 2018, my family as well as the Coughlins, my mother's sister's family, came. My grandfather Floodo and grandmother Sally, who was fighting cancer, made sure she could watch me graduate. Even though Sally was sick from all of the chemotherapy shots in her torso, she made the effort to see me graduate with flying colors. She sat down while everyone else stood up to clap as all of the students received diplomas. Despite the graduation taking place during the spring, which was warm, Sally still wore her winter coat because she was cold and weak from her battle with cancer.

They were all proud to see me accept my diploma and exit the education system. Even though she spent two years battling cancer, I knew Sally loved all of her grandkids and would do anything to see us graduate from college and into the work environment.

I felt like that was the most important day of my life, although it was a bit dark and gloomy during the morning. I knew that even though I had a lot of problems with some of the students in that college, my family was proud. My parents were especially proud, having been told by those specialists I wouldn't graduate high school, let alone college. Well, I proved those specialists wrong. We all went to the restaurant I went to on Saint Patrick's Day during my senior year. The waitress recognized me as we all sat down, and she congratulated me on graduating from college.

Two moments from Sammy's graduation will live with me forever. The first was watching my mother, Sally, struggling through her cancer treatments knowing the end was near but insisting on watching Sammy march across the stage and earn his college degree. Her treatment for bile duct cancer included tubes coming out of her stomach to drain fluids, which helped keep her alive. She would spend most of her waking hours in bed or in a comfortable chair. Two hours in a tent sitting on a folding metal chair on a cold wet May morning were not ideal conditions for Sally.

Jane and I were up on the graduation stage as members of the board of trustees for the college. We were so proud of Sammy, and we both came forward and joined the president to award his diploma. Through my tears, I couldn't see Sally in her seat and was devastated that she was not there for the big moment. Then I looked outside the tent in the rain and saw her frail body hunched over standing under an umbrella held by Uncle Terry. She couldn't sit, but she wouldn't miss that moment. The goal of Sammy's graduation fueled her through a painful year plus, and she was pouring tears in celebration of Sammy's big day.

The other moment to celebrate was the cheer that went up when Sammy's name was announced at the ceremony. The women on his basketball team made some noise for the big guy, and that was so uplifting. Sammy had connected with peers who appreciated him and made sure they were at the graduation to celebrate his accomplishment. Between Sally and the basketball team's reaction, the graduation will be one of the great lifetime memories for all the right reasons.

—Dad, Sam Flood

After college, the next step was to hunt for the right career and a place to live on my own. The next few chapters will discuss what I've been up to since I graduated college, which was not an easy process.

LIFE LESSONS

Pick up verbal and nonverbal cues.

Find a safe and quiet place to work.

Engage in other activities.

Don't demand respect.

Don't find love; let love find you first.

Be thankful for how far you've come.

— Chapter 7: —
After My College Graduation

After I graduated from Mitchell College, I was accepted to Broad Futures, an internship program in Washington D. C. for people with learning disabilities. I spent my summer of 2018 relaxing in our newly built summer home in Jamestown, Rhode Island, and preparing for the Small Business Administration internship to begin. I did go through some life lessons back home beforehand.

Off to the Races

My post-college life started with a trip to Baltimore for the Preakness Stakes in May 2018. I'd always heard about the big party scene at the Preakness and had attended the Belmont two times, including the year American Pharoah won the Triple Crown in 2015. The Belmont was a mass of people, loud and crazy. Dad told me the Preakness was even crazier and said they call it the "People's Party."

Honestly I was more excited about going to Baltimore to visit another city. I love exploring cities. When my parents used to ask me where I wanted to go for spring break, I always picked a city. I'd gone to Boston, Philadelphia, Washington D.C., and Charleston. I didn't tell Dad, but the opportunity to see Baltimore was a much bigger deal than watching another horse race. For a guy who hated chaos as a kid, the mashup of buildings and people somehow fascinates me. Someday I want to live in a small city and experience the city life. Since I don't drive, being able to walk everywhere or take a train or subway appeals to me. Cities have people, lots of people, and even though I don't talk a ton, I like being around people.

I explored Baltimore with Mom and got the feeling it was a city that could work for me. It was smaller than NYC and Boston but still had the water and mix of buildings. The challenge even to this day is finding a job and a life that works in one of these smaller cities. I want to live near the family but want my own place, my own space.

Back to the horse race and the Preakness. It was a party, and the track was crazy with live bands and DJs cranking out music. After the race, it was chaos during "the escape," trying to get through the people and the traffic and to the train back north. Because of my dad's job with NBC, we had our own SUV with a police escort, and I rode shotgun.

As we pulled out behind the policeman on his motorcycle, the SUV driver handed me her phone and asked me to make a film of the escape. She kept bossing me around and telling me where to point the camera. It was weird; she kept looking away from the road in front of her as drunk people wove their way around the car.

I finally snapped at her and told her to watch the road and pay attention to her job. I was afraid that I'd acted a bit bossy with a lady I'd never met, but everyone in the car thanked me for making the ride safer. It reminded me that I have a voice and need to speak up when something doesn't feel right. Sometimes people think I am in Sammyland and not aware of what is happening around me. The reality is I know what is going on and just don't always want to get in the middle of conversations. My comments to the driver made me feel good about being a responsible college graduate ready to speak up when needed.

> The transition from college to the adult world can be challenging for anyone. Many of the recent graduates arrive at NBC figuring out where they fit in this new world. For someone like Sammy, it is a bit more complicated. He can't always read the verbal and nonverbal cues. As parents, we make sure he understands the agenda and when we are being sarcastic.
>
> Post-Mitchell-College Sammy was more confident and had lost the anger and frustration that would occasionally bubble to the surface and create conflict. The Preakness car ride was a moment where you could see he was engaged and willing to speak up. In the past, Sammy would have shut down and shut out people around him after navigating a day of chaos and noise at the track. Instead, when he climbed into a car with five of my colleagues, he answered questions and was part of the conversation. This was a new step for him—in the past, we would need to insert ourselves in the conversations to engage Sammy in these settings. When Sammy told the driver to pay attention and focus on the road, it was a special moment. One of my colleagues commented how impressed he was with how Sammy handled the situation and how well he communicated. Most Sammy conversations with my colleagues had been hostage situations with one-word answers.
>
> **—Dad, Sam Flood**

I spent the remainder of the summer enjoying swims, golf, boat rides, and family time. The family time was even more important as my grandmother was in the battle for her life against cancer.

Family Tragedy in the Fall of 2018

Sally was diagnosed with a tumor around her liver (bile duct) in the winter of 2016, and she was told that she only had a year to live. We spent what was supposed to be her final Christmas, in 2016, in Jamestown, but Sally was able to make it through the Winter Break and, as always, exceeded expectations. But as the years passed, her battle with cancer only weakened her. Sally grew frailer, and she had to be cared for during most of 2018. Worse, Sally had to have needles or syringes injected into her torso all day to deliver her medicine or drain fluids. Sally would spend most of her days sitting in her family room, watching TV and sleeping, when her cancer advanced. But like for my graduation, Sally always rallied and made it out of the house for short visits with people. She hated being sick and loved life and people.

I would visit Sally every day. I was hoping she'd make it through. But Dad always told me that sometimes we have to say goodbye to our family members, and Mom had already lost her parents. Dad said our job was to carry those relatives in our hearts and to represent them in our lives. In early September 2018, I saw Sally lying on her bed, wasting away as Floodo and my dad helped keep her comfortable. I was afraid that when I left Jamestown that day, I never would see Sally alive again. I didn't tell Mom or Dad; I just kept saying, "Sally is going to be okay, right?" But deep down I knew she was not going to be with us much longer. Sadly, I knew I might lose an important person in our family.

In September of 2018, my dad received a call from his sister, saying that Sally passed away.

Sally was one of the most important people not only in my life, but also in the lives of the entire Flood family. She and Floodo had a lot of fun stories to tell about my dad's childhood as well as Uncle Dick's and Aunt Kassy's youth. When we were kids and my parents went out of town for a vacation or business trip, Sally was the one who took care of Eliza and me. She always made me feel like I was the most important person in the world and made me forget my problems. Sally believed in me and wanted to see my success in life.

Sally and Floodo would come every Christmas and give us a lot of love and presents. Every Christmas Eve, we would have a roast beef dinner together and tell a lot of funny stories. One of my favorites was when Sally promised to bring the cake to my christening in New Jersey. She was living at Salisbury School about two hours from our house. Apparently Sally bragged about how great the bakery was in town, and she insisted on supplying the cake for the twenty-five people. When she pulled into our driveway, she realized she had left the cake in the kitchen in Connecticut. They called a cab back in Connecticut and had a driver bring the cake to our house. Everyone joked that it was the most expensive cake in history. Thinking about her commitment to getting the cake to the party and the cake's cab ride makes me laugh. Christmas was so memorable telling stories by the Christmas tree and having coffee and breakfast. Now Christmas just isn't the same without Sally around. But as always, my family is accepting of what is the new normal. And besides, the Coughlins and Cahills always come over to our house every Christmas Eve to give us presents, and we give them presents.

Sally's declining health and passing had an emotional impact on Sammy. His hopeful statements were not based in reality, and we used to protect him from bad news. There was no use in protecting Sammy from the reality of Sally's situation. By the end of the summer, he was more comfortable talking with her and aware of the inev-

itable. I think he finally understood the importance and commitment of Sally fighting to attend his big day at the Mitchell graduation.
—Dad, Sam Flood

The Flood side of the family was saddened by Sally's death, and so my family and I spent the entire fall, from October to November, trying to help Floodo recover from Sally's death. This was the first time I saw Floodo sobbing. It must be hard to lose a wife or husband because of how much time they've spent together during their marriage, and Floodo took it pretty hard. We did whatever we could to help him through the worst time of his life. We took regular trips to Newport and having a few beers and bar food with him.

Back Pains

During my fall break, I began to walk around town often, mainly because of a back injury I received in which my spine was out of place and a bit crooked because I was out of shape. I spent the first week walking around like Quasimodo from *The Hunchback of Notre Dame* or Igor from *Frankenstein*. And every time I walked, every time I tried to stand up, I was in a catastrophic amount of pain. One time when my mom and I were walking out of the mall, some woman gave me a surprised look as I walked all crooked like a hunchback. I felt I could have yelled, "What!? You've never seen a guy with a crooked back before?" like that one episode from *Family Guy* when Joe, who was one of Peter's friends and used a wheelchair, noticed that some blowup dolls in a porn store were staring at him, and he yelled, "What, you've never seen a handicapped man before?"

My mom decided to take me to Dr. J, who was a chiropractor specializing in neck and back pains.

As we arrived at Dr. J's office, he was able to realign my spine. Dr. J told me my spine was out of alignment because I had gained a little gut that turned my spine all disjointed. I guess after my college run, I didn't know what to do with my life so I just played on my PlayStation 4 and ate a lot of junk food without any exercise, little realizing what would happen to my back. Without a schedule to guide me, I just didn't know what to do with my time other than just play video games, read, eat, and sleep.

When Dad found out my back fell out of alignment because I had a gut and was out of shape, he fat shamed me, and I felt a little embarrassed. The more Dad insulted me, the more I felt he was bullying me. But he kept on insulting me about my gut until I decided to start working out by walking and lifting weights. I know Dad was just trying to help me be in better shape, but the way he talked about my gut, it felt like he was acting like one of those bullies who harassed me back at Maplebrook. And I guess his making fun of me was kind of karma for how I had humiliated Crosby, although that dog has been getting in shape recently.

Bergen County Writers Guild

In September of 2018, I joined the Bergen County Writers Guild, and my Uncle Terry took me to my first workshop. At first, I thought it was just a group of writers around Terry's age, but when I arrived at the workshop, I saw people around my age or in their twenties or thirties. The Guild members included Jeff, who was a high school history teacher interested in *Star Wars*; Eresh, a transgender college woman, Hannah, who was Asian and wrote her own sci-fi story about a little girl learning to be a space magician; Yale, a horror writer and my closest friend; AJ, a poet; Maurice, the oldest of our gang who had written some novels of his own; and Ray, the leader of the guild, who had a keen interest in anime. We all became friends because of our interests in geek culture such as comics, movies, video games, and books. The Writer's Guild met every Wednesday, and we took turns reading the other writers' stories and making critiques about what we liked and what we didn't like. We also went out to restaurants sometimes for fun.

One time, the gang and I went to Jeff's house for a holiday party where we watched *Indiana Jones* movies. Jeff had invited some of his friends as well as some of the writers' workshop members, including me. It was the first time that I was at Jeff's house. Although it was small, I did like how he had a lot of comic books, DVDs of *Star Wars*, Marvel movies, DC movies, *The Lord of the Rings*, and *Harry Potter*. Plus, he had a nice basement with a flat-screen TV and a bar. We all had a fun time as we ate pizza, drank beer and soda, and watched *Indiana Jones* movies.

> The writers' workshop was a gift to Sammy. It allowed him to have an outlet where he was part of something beyond his immediate family. He was proud to have his own group and always was eager to head off to the meetings at Barnes and Noble. In the new world of folks working from home, there will be even more need for everyone to find affinity groups outside the office. We were thrilled to watch Sammy forge friendships and find some like minds to share time and activities. He was lucky to have Uncle Terry open that door and help guide Sammy into the writers guild. Terry was a sci-fi guy to Sammy's fantasy novels. Together they bonded over keyboards, chicken wings, and beer.
>
> **—Dad, Sam Flood, and Mom, Jane Flood**

We became friends with each other. Being together was not just meeting to talk about writing. The writer's workshop made me feel I was a part of something. I felt comfortable as we all talked about comics, movies, video games, and books. In the past, mainly during my Eagle Hill days, it was not okay for me to talk about these things, and I felt ashamed. We also got together on a few occasions for holiday celebrations, dinners, movies, and just a simple drink at a bar.

LIFE LESSONS

The people you love will one day be gone.

There's a place to make new friends waiting outside of your own world.

Chapter 8:
Internship in Washington, D.C.

At the start of 2019, my parents drove me to Washington, D. C. for my internship with Broad Futures, a program that helps kids with learning disabilities find their place in the work environment. Broad Futures started out when Carolyn Jeppsen and her friends Diana and Brad were talking in a coffee shop in Washington, D.C., about how their kids were having difficulty finding a full-time job because of their learning disabilities. They decided to create an organization that helps kids with learning differences find a job by teaching them how to function within the work environment.

I learned about Broad Futures during my senior year in college. Ted, who was working at the admissions office at Mitchell, was talking to me about what I wanted to do after graduation. He said Broad Futures would be perfect for a guy like me. Ted explained that once I graduated, I would have a tough time finding a job because of my learning disabilities. He told me that there was a summer internship in Broad Futures, but I didn't apply because there weren't any opportunities in graphic design. I thought since my degree was in graphic design, my career needed to be in a related field. I eventually decided to take the 2019 winter course at

Broad Futures and was willing to look at any type of job. I realized that it was time to get into the work world.

During my first two weeks in Washington, D.C., I took acting classes geared toward having an internship at the Broad Futures campus at George Washington University. I learned a lot about what to do and what not to do while working. Sometimes at the end of a session, our drama instructor, Raymond, had us reenact certain moments that might happen in the office or even at home. This process of role playing helped us prepare to manage situations when we set out in the real world.

Other times, we ended our sessions with yoga. Shauna, our instructor, taught us various ways of stretching and meditating. She said that yoga helped stretch out our muscles after sitting at a desk all day at work. Unfortunately, I'm not a very flexible man as I usually act out of sync with the rest of the group due to my long body. My dad jokes I'm not very flexible physically or with my schedule.

During one yoga class, when the students were meditating, I made a funny "Ommmmm" sound like I was vibrating during an earthquake. One of the students, Alec, was annoyed by my meditation sound. I told Alec that I was just having a little fun, and he replied by telling me not to goof off during yoga. He said yoga is a way of life and should not be taken as a joke. It was one more reminder that I need to be aware of how my actions impact those around me. (That being said, chill, dude.)

Sometimes during our two-week training program, we did group projects, such as writing on a very big poster board about what Broad Futures really represents. I wrote down my experiences with both Broad Futures and Washington, D. C. with words including *Chick-Fil-A*, *DuPont Circle*, *Yoga*, *Drama*, and *International Student Housing*. I really wanted to show the program how much the city and Broad Futures meant to me, as they helped me learn not only how to function within the work environment but also to function in and around the city itself.

International Student Housing

I lived in a dorm called International Student Housing, a facility where people, mainly students and interns from different countries around the world, stayed while they attended class or completed internships. My roommate was Dickson, a student from Ghana, Africa, who was studying for a master's degree in teaching. He and I became friends and hung out, mainly during breakfast and dinner and later when Dickson was doing homework. But over time, I felt I needed a single room because Dickson stayed up late, kept the light on so he could study for whatever exam he had the next day, or snored loudly like a grizzly bear and wouldn't let me keep the A/C running when I felt hot in our room. Dickson told me that it's hot back in Ghana, and he was used to that kind of weather. I guess the lesson was that everyone has different comfort levels. Some like it hot.

One time during Mardi Gras, I went back to the dorm after I had just hung out with my mom during the weekend in D.C., and Dickson put a purple hat from the celebration on me and wanted me to party with him. I was worn out from my Friday meetings, where we go over our internships with Broad Futures, and my time out with mom. I only hung out with Dickson for a few minutes before I went back to my room to shower. I left Dickson to hang out with my other friends in the dorm.

He was hurt by the fact that I left him on his own and claimed that I was being a terrible friend. He said, "Is it because I'm black?" He said I wasn't hanging out with him because of his Ethiopian background.

I have nothing against people from different ethnic backgrounds. I told him, "What about the people you hang out with, aren't they your friends?"

Dickson said, "They're my classmates from the college I go to, not my friends." He thought that because I was his roommate, he and I were best friends.

But I'd learned my lesson from Josh back at Mitchell College that sometimes roommates don't have to be friends. I said, "Sometimes roommates don't have to be friends."

Dickson started crying after what I said. We went to sleep completely silent toward each other like those comedy movies where the two buddies don't talk to each other after they have a bad fight.

The next day, I told my mom about my argument with Dickson, and she said that maybe he was just having a difficult time picking up social cues. People, no matter their background, often don't understand how a person is feeling or thinking, and they misinterpret situations.

I apologized to Dickson about what had happened and how we both have a difficult time picking up social cues.

In February of 2019, the Bodens, who were friends of my parents in Jamestown, Rhode Island, invited me to a Super Bowl party. The Bodens own a house in a suburb area outside of Washington, D. C. Originally I was planning on watching the Super Bowl with my new friends within the common area, but my dad suggested I go to the Super Bowl party at the Bodens' house. I asked Dickson what his Super Bowl plan was, and he said that he'd never watched the game before. Having grown up in Ghana, Dickson had never had the experience of a Super Bowl party, which is an unofficial American Holiday. So I offered to take him to the party at the Bodens' house. We took an Uber, and Dickson and I watched the game with Mr. and Mrs. Boden and their sons, James and Evan. James started to get along with Dickson quite well as James learned a lot about the culture of Ghana. Dickson was impressed by not only the actual game but the commercials as well, which, in my opinion are the best part of the SuperBowl.

When I first met Dickson, I wasn't ready to get along with him because of my past experience with Josh back at Mitchell College. I was worried that Dickson would neglect me and treat me like a roommate, not a friend. But the more time Dickson and I spent time together, the more we became friends. Sure, we made some mistakes, but we found a way to forgive each other. To quote Donkey from *Shrek*, "That's what friends do; they forgive each other."

Some of my other friends in the International dorm were Sofia, a thin blonde woman from Germany; Orla, a dark-haired Irish woman from Oregon; Bat Chan, a twenty-three-year old student from Mongolia; Manuel, who was from Liechtenstein; and Phillip, a dark-haired guy from France. They had come to Washington to intern for companies, study courses from their native countries, or attend colleges in the city.

I also made some friends who were from the Broad Futures Program, Steve and John. Some of the Broad Futures students stayed in International Student Housing because they were from states far away from Washington, D. C. Steve, John, and I usually spent most of our time together during the Friday Broad Future meetings, which focused on what we'd learned during our internships that week. We usually had lunch together at the Au Bon Pain sandwich store that's right next to the Broad Futures classroom. Other times, we go to the Chick-Fil-A in the cafeteria at George Washington University. I liked Chick-Fil-A more than Au Bon Pain—fried food always wins. Plus, I invented a new dipping sauce, as I'd dip the nuggets and/or waffle fries into my vanilla milkshake. Gross? Maybe. But this was me living as an independent adult in a city hundreds of miles from my family. If my biggest mistake was dipping chicken into a milkshake, it doesn't seem that bad.

During my time in International Student Housing, I attended three ethnic parties celebrating various cultures. The first party I went to was an Indian party where Dickson was dressed in white traditional Indian robes. He and I danced around a bit in a circle, which is Indian tradition. A TV screen played the most popular Bollywood music videos, including the Tunak Tunak Tun song.

The next party, in early March, was a Japanese party. Dickson wasn't there because he was working on an assignment, so I went to the party without him. The Japanese party was fascinating, not just because of the food, but also because of games like Kendrama, where you try to get the ball on a string to land on either end of a mallet. I also learned kanji, a Japanese writing style where you draw symbols which could translate into a single word. For example, I drew the kanji symbols for fire, water, wind, wood, earth, light, snow, and lightning.

The third party I went to in late March was an Ethiopian party that Dickson and his friends hosted because of their African heritage. I thought of going to the party to support Dickson, but Uncle Terry and Aunt Kathryn were visiting Washington, D.C. that weekend during the party. I told Dickson that my relatives were coming, and I had to take them around DuPont Circle during the evening. But Dickson said I had to go to the party to show my support for him. I told Terry and Kathryn about the Ethiopian party, and they said that they would meet me for dinner at around 6:30 PM. So I went to the party early that day to hang out with Dickson. As the party was going on, I kept getting texts from Terry asking me, "Where are you, Bum?" So I told my roommate that my relatives were expecting me and left the party. I never got to enjoy some of the Ethiopian food like injera, wat, tibs, kitfo, ful, and beyaynatu.

Exploring Washington, D.C.

When I first arrived in Washington, D.C., I was amazed by the multicultural restaurants, book stores, museums, and historical sites. Whenever my sister, parents, or other relatives came to visit me on weekends, we would go to museums and historical sites such as the Lincoln Memorial, Museum of Natural History, Museum of African American History, The Washington Monument, the White House gates, or the cherry blossom peak. One time when my Uncle Terry and Aunt Kathryn came to visit me, we took pictures of the cherry blossom peak where tourists gather every spring. After we took our pictures, we went to see the memorial for all those who had died during our country's wars. But when I got back to my dorm room, I realized that I had gotten a severe sunburn on my shoulders. Maybe I should have put sunscreen on before I went sightseeing in the capital. Apparently one more lesson of living on my own... no mom or dad to nag me to put on sunscreen. Perhaps they weren't nags at all but trying to help. Lesson learned.

Broad Futures took the interns to the Museum of African American History one Friday during Black History Month. We learned how African tribes were captured and enslaved by European explorers during the sixteenth century. We also saw how African Americans struggled through the history of our country, how they were treated as slaves in the Confederate States of America, and then how they were treated as second-class citizens during the 1950s and 1960s leading Dr. Martin Luther King Jr. to deliver his "I Have a Dream" speech. My favorite part in the Museum of African American History were the displays of famous African American stars during their rise in the 1970s and 1980s.

My sister gave me a coupon for a French restaurant in the capital called Le Diplomate, and it was the first time I had snails; they were so good. I went out to a lot of restaurants in Washington D.C., but my favorites were Shake Shack, Chick-Fil-A, Le Diplomate, Rakuya, Dupont Pizza, Bedrock Billiards, and Peking Garden. The only minor problem I had with D. C. is that I could not find any. But I found a really good comic book store called Fantom Comics in DuPont Circle. It had a decent category of graphic novels and some manga. I would go there whenever I had the day off from work or in the afternoon during my weekdays.

I also went to Georgetown, another district in Washington, D.C., on weekends and would just wander around the area and go to some of the restaurants such as 90 Seconds Pizza, Thunder Burger and Bar, and America Eats. Georgetown also has an amazing old-school movie theater where my sister's friend, Ted, took me to see *Captain Marvel*. The interior of the theater was huge. After the movie, I spotted a Hershey's Ice Cream store and had ice cream. Whenever I went to Georgetown, I would just eat and look at the Potomac River. I also enjoyed the Amazon bookstore within that area and bought some graphic novels and normal books in case I ran out of reading material. Just like the main city, Georgetown looks beautiful during the spring. I felt like Georgetown was the place I might have lived in or gone to college, despite the fact that it is extremely expensive. I'm not sure Georgetown would have accepted me as a student, but I could have added to the diversity of learners on campus. My curiosity and love of reading opens doors for me, but at age nineteen, I was far from ready for a place like Georgetown University.

Internships have evolved through the years and now are a more formal part of people's career training. It used to be that interns were hired because of who they knew or where they went to college. Fortunately the process has changed, and doors are open for more people with diverse backgrounds. Unfortunately that is not true for young adults like Sammy who have learning differences. Broad Futures is a blessing for this slice of society.

We were lucky to watch Sammy evolve and function in Washington, D.C. The Broad Futures training program gets the interns ready to function inside a business and supports the companies and the interns every day. The daily communication with the intern's advisor solves problems before they become major issues. The simple phone distraction example with Sammy shows the value of constant communication. More people entering the workforce could use guidance from a program like Broad Futures.

We were so impressed by Carolyn Jeppesen's leadership and concept that we joined the Broad Futures board. We are eager to create an even bigger program that can hopefully lead to full-time work for more Sammy Floods. Diversity in the workplace is an important evolution, and ideally, Broad Futures can play a major role in growing this space for youdeng adults with learning differences.

—Dad, Sam Flood, and Mom, Jane Flood

Working for APSE

Before I departed for Washington, I learned that President Trump ordered a governmental shutdown, which included the Small Business Administration. So instead of working at the SBA, my first internship was with APSE, the Association for People Supporting Employment in Derwood, Maryland.

The work I did for APSE was tiring but good. I organized computer files, made posters for certain events, and did data entry on how much the company spent over the year. When I first started working, I was often distracted and was on my phone a lot. I would browse through the internet on pictures of my favorite games, and sometimes I watched YouTube videos that made a lot of noise, which distracted my coworkers.

Alexa, my advisor from Broad Futures, called me to say that I should spend less time on my phone and focus on work. She said I could goof off on my phone during lunch break or sometimes before work begins if I arrived early.

I guess I'm part of the era where people like me usually get distracted on their smartphones so they can watch the latest YouTube or TikTok videos, post photos on Twitter, Instagram, or Tumblr, and post the latest comments or posts on Twitter, Facebook, and Instagram. And seeing how I have ADHD, this is worse for me as I would be on my phone for days on end like a drug addict. I did what Alexa recommended, and I stopped going on my phone during work. As it turns out, I was able to complete assignments without getting distracted. So, big work lesson number one was to stay focused on the job and not allow the phone to be a distraction.

But there was another problem that reared its ugly head. Some intern who was on our Broad Futures text chain was texting a lot of political stuff about Donald Trump and what was going on in Congress. I'd learned there are three things you should never talk about during dinner, a party, class, or work. 1. Don't talk about money. 2. Don't talk about religion. 3. Don't talk about politics. But that student didn't get the memo and decided to become one of those political trolls and start harassing us. I couldn't take it anymore, so one Thursday, I called Alexa and told her about the text troll who'd been bringing politics into our conversations. The next day during our Friday meeting, Carolyn, the head of the program, gave us a lecture on how you should never bring up politics during work because it's more of a personal matter, like religion and money. Some of the students felt I tattled on the troll, but I was trying to put a stop to it the best way I could think of. After it quieted down, Carolyn said I did the right thing by bringing the issue to her attention.

Speaking of lunch break, the refrigerator only had ham and salad. I tried making a ham sandwich with gluten-free bread, but it did not taste good. Then I tried ordering Chinese food the next day using my credit card. After I got home from work, my dad called me to see how many meals I used the credit card for and suggested that I make my own lunch. As you can see earlier in this chapter, I liked to go out to eat a lot. So for the next three months, every Sunday, I would buy a cooked chicken from the Safeway market and store the chicken in the refrigerator in the laundry room at the dorm. Monday, I would lug it to work and keep it in the company fridge. The lunch order for the next four days was chicken, chicken, chicken, and chicken. Great variety for a guy who loves change.

Working for APSE was the first time I commuted to work. I would take the Metro from DuPont Circle to Rockville, MD, where the APSE office was located. At first, it was a little confusing to get on and off the train, and I was a bit afraid that I would end up in the wrong place. But over time, I got the hang of the commute and knew where I was going. I started to develop this routine where every Sunday, I would go to the subway station underneath DuPont Circle and buy myself a weekly train pass so I could go in and out of the subway and get on the train. As a bonus, sometimes I rode the Metro to Chinatown or the Smithsonian Museums of Natural History, American History, Art, and

Space. But there were a lot of passengers, and I did make a few mistakes on the subway.

One day after I was finished with work, I got on the subway, and an African American man pointed at me as I got on my seat. I tried to look out the window in order to avoid him. But as he got to his spot, he pointed his fingers at me like he was holding a gun and said, "Bang, stay back, Nazi." I didn't know why he would think I'm a Nazi. I texted my mom about this, and she said, "He must have a lot of mental issues, and it's best if you don't make eye contact with him."

Another time when I was going home from work, a bunch of kids were messing around as they ran around the subway car. One of them was letting the door slam him whenever it automatically opened and closed. I would try to tell him to stop because he was crushing his nuts, but I decided not to get involved in it and let the authorities deal with him. But his friends, who were standing in the emergency exit door in another car, were asking me to open the door for them so they could meet up with their friend. I got up and told them to read the sign that says, "Don't open." But they didn't listen to me. Sometimes whenever I think about those kids messing around in the subway, I wish I had written them a note on my smartphone that read, "Do they not teach English in whatever school you go to? Because I'm pretty sure it says, 'Do Not Open.'" I asked one of the subway workers if I could open the door, and he said I was not supposed to open the door. I realized that it's best to just keep to myself whenever I'm in a large or crowded city and avoid these problems altogether.

Three Week Break

After I completed my APSE internship, I went back to Ridgewood for three weeks, and I hung around the house, doing whatever I could to entertain myself. Often, I was catching up on my PlayStation 4 Pro because it had been four months since I played any video games on my home console. After a couple of weeks, I got bored and was ready to go back to work. You can only play so many video games.

My mom went to see *Avengers Endgame*, a superhero movie. My mom would not shut up. She just kept asking me questions during the movie, like "Who's the kid?" "Who's that guy?" "What's going on?" That's because she had never seen any of the movies from the Marvel Cinematic Universe.

After the movie, I went to a Barnes and Noble and just for laughs, I texted my friends at the writers workshop, spoiling the Avengers Endgame by texting things like "Spoiler Alert" "Black Widow died" "Iron Man died" and "Thanos dies," all events that occurred in the movie.

The writers who had not seen the movie, including Uncle Terry, did not like my spoiling it for them. A part of me forced me to spoil the movie for my friends. I didn't want to tell them the untold parts of *Endgame*, but I felt like something was controlling me. In my head, I felt like I was giggling as I was about to fire a flaming crossbow bolt toward someone, and I said, "I'm going to do it" even though some Orc with a British accent said, "Don't you do it."

This was a good lesson in how not to be a jerk. Clearly I'd crossed the line, and it had a negative impact with my friends. I decided to respect other people and not spoil movie endings going forward.

Also during the break, my mom took me to do yoga with her friends in a nearby town called Glenrock. I had done yoga every Friday during my internship with Broad Futures because it was mandatory. I did not enjoy yoga mainly because my body wasn't designed to stretch, and we did a lot of stretching exercises. I felt I was the one black sheep in Mom's yoga group seeing how I was twenty-five, and my mom's friends were all in their late forties and early fifties. After all of my yoga classes, I preferred to take long walks.

Working for the Small Business Administration

I went back to Washington, D. C. to do my Small Business Administration internship. The work I did for the SBA kept me extremely busy: organizing computer files, going over the company's folders, making copies of certain company documents, doing observatory checks on company members' phone numbers and email accounts, and observing and doing data entry on how much the company was spending over the year.

My supervisor, Catalina, gave me these assignments. Most of the time, work was brutal and I felt like I was going to pass into a coma at any second. Now I know what it's like for most employees to work in a cubicle five days a week from 7 A.M. to 6 P.M. But I found a way to make sure work isn't so tedious. I'd bring a piece of candy like fresh mint, a piece of caramel, or butterscotch with me to work and eat it in order to both keep my mind focused and to keep myself energized. Sometimes I'd take some fruit-flavored Tootsie rolls from the couch outside of Catalina's office and eat those too.

I had some fun memories about my time with the Small Business Administration, like when some of the people who worked there took me to see a Washington Nationals baseball game at Nationals Park in August of 2019. Trying to get to the baseball stadium was a pain. I had to take a train from DuPont all the way to National Park, but I got a little confused where my stop was supposed to be, and I was taken to a subway station in Alexandria, Virginia. After minutes of wandering from one nearby city to another and landing in Arlington, Virginia, I was like, "Screw it," and called an Uber to take me to Nationals Park. I finally arrived at Nationals Park and was able to watch six innings of the baseball game with my coworkers.

Although I did have a lot of fun working for the SBA, I did not enjoy the rest of my summer in Washington because the city was extremely hot and humid. I was sweating like a stuck pig most of the time. I remember coming home from work, buying a ton of seltzer water and soda for my dorm room, and just keeping the A/C turned to a low temperature. Part of me felt it was a mistake taking a summer internship within Washington, D. C. because of the heat. My parents told me it was all a part of being an adult, having to work during the summer and having little to no week-end breaks.

At the SBA, people in the area of my cubicle, Catalina included, threw me a going-away party as my internship was ending. I guess it was my reward for helping them out during my entire summer internship and being their closest friend. As a going-away present, they gave me a large bag of fruit-flavored Tootsie rolls.

After My Internship

After my internship with the SBA was completed, my mom drove me back home to Ridgewood, and a few days later, we drove to Rhode Island to spend the final weeks of August. I'd spent seven months in Washington, D. C., from January to August. It was the first time that I learned how to live on my own in a city, and I pretty much enjoyed it. I learned how to take the subway to and from various locations and eat on my own at the many bars and restaurants. I made many friends at both the International Student Housing and Broad Futures and did a lot of fun events with them. I saw many great sites and bookstores, and I learned to commute on my own with the help of Uber. I was influenced by the different cultures in DuPont Circle as well as by International Student Housing, where I went to three cultural parties, the Indian party, the Japanese party, and the African party. I can pretty much say 2019 was a great year even though a lot of it was spent in hot Washington, D.C.

LIFE LESSONS

Sometimes a job opens a window to grow.

Be sure to explore your surroundings so you can know the location of where you're living.

Don't spoil books or movies for others.

Chapter 9:
Before the Covid-19 shut down
(2019–2020)

After I completed my two summer internships in Washington, D.C., my parents and I decided I needed a full-time job, so we went on a job hunt during the fall. It was not an easy process.

The Troubling Job Hunt

My first attempt to get a job was working for Brown Brothers Harriman, an investment bank where Tim, aka Tinker, my dad's college friend, works. Even though I did my best in the job interview with Brown Brothers Harriman, they didn't hire me because they didn't have the right position to offer a person who has learning disabilities like mine. They were not ready to spend the time training me nor did they have the resources to get me up to speed.

My second attempt at finding a job was at Ernst and Young, the accounting firm. It was recommended for Broad Futures alumni who are looking to work for companies that are willing to help those with learning disabilities. I think I did a good job with the phone interview, and a few days later, when my Uncle Terry was taking me to a burger place, I received a phone call from Ernst and Young. They were willing to offer me a job, but when I told them I wanted one in accounting, they said I needed to have a degree in accounting. The caller gave me an offer to go to an accounting class, but my uncle suggested I do entry level work for EY. I received an automated call from a woman speaking, and I found it hard to focus on what she was saying. The whole conversation went wrong, and she hung up on me. It was a valuable lesson that I needed to be focused on the conversation and not be distracted by others during a phone call. Going forward, I vowed to let a call go to voicemail if I was in the wrong environment to conduct a business call. When we just answer phones wherever we are, it creates problems for getting a job.

The job market was difficult for me because I failed to connect with the people making the calls and doing the interviews. I practiced for the interviews with my parents, but it was different from the real interview setting. I'd give it my all in the interview, but then I wouldn't get a follow-up call or email, even though I gave them my contact information after I did the interview with them. It was very disheartening to get no response after getting my hopes up for a job. It felt a bit like high school when some schools rejected my application. But at least the schools said no—these companies never even bothered to contact me.

After my two failed attempts at landing full-time jobs in an office work environment, my mom suggested I get a part-time job with Barnes and Noble. I sent my resume and information to the store at the Riverside Mall. Days later, Adam from Barnes and Noble in Riverside called me and was willing to do an interview. I did a good job in the interview. I also sent my resume to the Barnes and Noble in Paramus. Days later, I received a phone call, but I thought it was a telemarketer, so I hung up. But then I realized that it was the Paramus Barnes and Noble offering me a job. I told my mom about it, but I'd forgotten the name of the person who had called me. She was upset with me and had me call the Riverside Barnes and Noble even though they told me to wait until they called me. I messed up that call, too.

In the summer of 2019, I saw a job opening for a restaurant in Jamestown called Simpatico. I spent the whole week preparing for the interview, and when I got to Simpatico, Rachael, the owner of the place, gave me an offer to be the front desk manager to help customers find their seats or make reservations if the tables were full. It was a perfect job for me. I have learned to be patient on the phone and am great with text and email. I was proud to have this new opportunity to work near our house in Rhode Island. Unfortunately, I never got the email or call telling me when I would train and start the job. I sent an email asking for guidance but got no response. I worked so hard on that interview and felt it was thrown back in my face like I was a joke. You get sensitive when you have learning differences and some people are afraid to communicate with you. I might be tall and deliberate in conversation but really want to be communicated with just like anyone else applying for work or school. Be honest with me—don't be afraid of me and treat me like an outcast.

We were not making any progress in the job hunt, so Dad wanted me to take accounting classes. No chance I was going back to school. I'd graduated from college and was done with school. I wanted to start using the pamphlet Broad Futures gave me, which recommended jobs for interns who'd completed the program. A few weeks later, my dad was able to get in contact with Broad Futures, and they were willing to work with NBC Sports to offer me an internship during the spring of 2020. But I never got to complete the internship, thanks to the pandemic that hit right when the program was going to start in March of 2020.

My Weekend in Charlotte

Even though I was having a difficult time with the job search process, I do have some fun memories of being with my family and my friends. During a weekend in mid-September, my dad took me to Charlotte, North Carolina, to watch a NASCAR race. I had some fun walking around a pond near the hotel and going to some stores and restaurants like a Game Spot and Blaze's Pizza. I wanted to go to a Cajun crawfish restaurant because I'd never had crawfish in my life. But Dad told me that these crawfish have been fished out of the murky river near the bayou and not from the sea.

My dad and I went to a bar near the hotel to meet some of his friends and watch football. I had plain wings and a burger and fries and drank beer while watching the game. I realized that this was what most guys my age did on weekends. It was pleasurable to escape the job search and have some fun, drinking beer, playing arcade games, watching football on the big screen, and feeling like one of the guys.

During the NASCAR race, I spent most of my time relaxing in a luxurious NBC van that had internet access and snacks. I was glued to my iPad while my dad broadcast the race. Sure, I watched some of the races in the stadium, but I preferred the comfy couches of the NBC van.

When Dad and I got home back to New Jersey, we told my mom about our time in Charlotte and of course the burger, wing, and fry combo I had. My mom thought it was unhealthy because I had a physical exam scheduled the week after, and she thought I should watch what I ate. Little did I know how right Mom was.

Time to get Physical

In late September 2019, My mom and I went to see Dr. Rooney for my physical. Unfortunately, a physical means getting your blood taken with a long needle . . . okay, the needle is not actually that long, but any needle freaks me out. I panicked so much that my mom had to hold my hand. I held her hand so hard I almost broke it, and it was very embarrassing to be an adult while acting like a ten-year-old child.

When I got home, Dad said he was embarrassed for me and I needed to grow up. I realized that Mom had been there for me every time we went to the doctor. One day, Mom won't be there at the doctor's office, so I need to man up and behave like an adult. It also reminded me how lucky I am to have a mother who is always there for me making sure I'm okay. It can't be easy for her to always be worried about me. Usually kids graduate college and head out on their own, and I realized I needed to accomplish that soon for Mom's sake.

Fortunately, two years later, I went to Quest diagnostics in Ridgewood and asked the woman taking my blood if I could look at my iPhone so I wouldn't have to look at the needle being injected into my skin and was able to watch YouTube which helped me not stress or worry so much about the process.

Back to the doctor drama of September 2019. Days after the appointment, Dr. Rooney told me that my cholesterol had spiked due to all the fried stuff I had been eating. My dad suggested I tone down the fried food and focus on eating green. Since then, I have gone on a salad side dish and a Cheerio breakfast diet. I usually have salad as a side dish for my lunches and some dinners. I rarely go out to my favorite restaurants like Tori Ramen, Jersey Mike Subs, and East Coast Burger since they have the chance to spike my cholesterol.

My dad told me to go to the local fitness center in our neighboring town of Glen Rock. I signed up for a two day per week course for two months at Volt Fitness. I had a personal trainer who taught me the basic workout techniques like weight lifting, push-ups, sit-ups, and running on the treadmill. Then my trainer and I were able to come up with new and more advanced workout techniques like pushing and pulling the weights from one end of the room to the other, boxing, climbing, ball lifting, and crunches. The more I worked out, the fitter I became. My gut shrank, and my muscles grew. Originally my mom and I had decided that I was going to end my sessions with Volt Fitness around January of 2021. But when I went to mail in the check to pay off my sessions, I decided to work out a little more.

Losing Floodo

In the fall of 2019, Floodo died from prostate cancer. The male Floods have a history of prostate cancer. Some get it young, like my dad in his late forties. Floodo and Uncle Dick got prostate cancer in their sixties. My Dad and Uncle Dick were lucky to recover by having their prostates removed. Floodo wasn't so lucky. His prostate went bad, and it was too late for a surgery to save him. He was okay during the first few stages of prostate cancer, but his fight was disappearing as he was losing his best friend and wife of more than sixty years to her own cancer. Despite Sally's passing, he was pretty calm as we spent the winter of 2018 celebrating Christmas together.

But when fall came around, Floodo's cancer had gotten much worse, and he wasn't getting any better. Dad spent the last days of September visiting Floodo just to be there during his final days. In October of 2019, Mom told me that Floodo passed away. Now all four grandparents were gone. I didn't really get to know Mom's parents since they died when I was really young, but Floodo and Sally were a big part of my life. It made me very sad to know we would no longer share time together. I now know how much Floodo helped get me into Eagle Hill School and how early on he had found Dr. Helpful in New York City. Those two connections changed my life for the better.

The Floods, the Brit Floods, and Fritzes spent the entire Thanksgiving week having a burial and memorial for Floodo. On Thanksgiving Day, I had my first taste of whisky, and I did not like it. The Friday after Thanksgiving, the whole family went to bury Floodo with Sally back in Boston. Afterward, we watched the Bruins Game with twenty family members and friends who loved Floodo. What better way to celebrate a hockey coach than by going to a game of the team he always rooted for? On the NBC telecast of the game, they did a whole tribute remembering Floodo. It was very touching to see how much of an impact Floodo left not only on the family, but also on all of his friends, students, and fellow teachers back when he was teacher, coach, and headmaster. Part of me felt that it was deja vu with the whole Flood family having to celebrate Thanksgiving after the death of a relative and go to his/her memorial service during Thanksgiving weekend. Just like with Sally the year before.

Christmas 2019 was the first holiday the family and I celebrated without Floodo and Sally. It was sad to know that we won't be able to have a Christmas where Floodo and Sally would come over during Christmas Eve, go to church on either the 24th or 25th, open stockings on Christmas Day and later presents, and have a Christmas roast dinner. But the Fritzes were willing to drive from Andover, Massachusetts, all the way to Ridgewood, New Jersey, to celebrate Christmas with us. We had coq au vin for lunch. For some reason, I was amused by the name and was a bit childish making jokes but hey, we needed to lighten the mood. Then the Fritzes left to go celebrate the holidays with Uncle Tom's side of the family, and my family and I went to Rhode Island to celebrate the rest of the holiday season up until New Year's Eve.

Holiday Season of 2019

During the 2019 holiday season, my friends from the writers workshop and I went to a park in the Paramus area. We did many fun activities such as enjoying the carousel (even though we were too big for it), riding on the train, even though we were too big for it, also, and relaxing at Barnes and Noble.

I also went to Jeff's holiday party to watch the *Star Wars Holiday Special*, and we riffed on that. We watched *Revenge of the Sith*, also in Jeff's basement, which had a bar. The gang and I made some funny comments during the movie such as "Go to the Jedi Temple at a brisk pace," and "Lord Sidious promised us peace and General Tso Chicken" (right before Anakin killed the last of the Separatists, who were a Chinese stereotype).

On December 19, 2019, Jeff, AJ, and I went to see the world premiere of *Rise of Skywalker*. I remember that the entire movie theater was packed with *Star Wars* cosplayers (people who dress up as a fictional character) and people wearing *Star Wars* merchandise. I enjoyed the fight scenes and new locations of the movie although AJ said he felt the bit about Emperor Palpatine being Rey's Grandfather was pretty stupid, and Jeff thought the plot was like a video game with the characters going from point A to point B in order to find a plot device. After I got home from the movie theater, my mom's friends from the book club asked me to spoil the movie, but I just told them that Emperor Palpatine was Rey's Grandfather. Part of me felt that I could have done what Homer Simpson did when he saw *Empire Strikes Back*, as I would have said after watching *Rise of Skywalker*: "Who would have thought that Emperor Palpatine was Rey's Grandfather?"

I went to Jeff's house for his New Year's Eve party. I thought that most or some of the writers workshop members would be coming, but when I got there, it was only five people, Jeff included, who were all Jeff's friends from his high school years. We spent New Year's Eve watching the *Super Girl* movie, which was awful in my opinion with its terrible special effects, mishandled story, and stilted acting. Later we watched one episode of *Chip N Dale Rescue Rangers* and one episode of *Darkwing Duck* on Jeff's Disney Plus account, and then it was time to watch the ball drop to welcome in 2020.

While I made a toast to how much 2019 was a great year for me since I was able to go to Washington, D. C. for seven months to do two internships, Jeff made another toast saying, "Here's to a lousy year of me dealing with health issues and a terrible breakup. And may 2020 be a better year for me." That did not come true, thanks to Covid.

This group of friends was really important to me and made me feel like I was part of something. It was great to go to my own social events and not be hanging with my parents. The writers workshop had a mix of people that I related to and really made me feel I belonged. It was a first for me outside of a school setting, and I felt like a real adult.

Hot Tea Jeans

During February of 2020, AJ told the writer's workshop that she was transferring to Virginia for her new job. AJ's original company had gone into bankruptcy, and many employees lost their jobs, including her. She was sad about it, so we hugged her. In the middle of the hug, her hot tea spilled all over my pants, ruining my jeans, and I screamed in pain. I spent the entire workshop session with tea-stained jeans. I will always associate AJ's departure with tea spilling on my jeans. After that tea event, the group decided we should support AJ by hanging out with her before she left for Virginia.

Also in February 2020, Uncle Terry, Jeff, and Yale, members of the writers' workshop, took AJ and me to a bar in Bergen County. I made sure to order beer and not tea. Terry, Jeff, and Yale order double fried wings, while I ordered the single fried wings. When Terry asked me about it, I told him that I had to watch my cholesterol because during my 2019 physical checkup, my doctor told me that my cholesterol level had spiked and I had to be careful with how much fried food and ice cream I ate. Terry called me a wimp and said while mimicking my voice, "Oh, my God, I have to watch my cholesterol." Weeks later, my mom had to remind him about my cholesterol problem when we paid a visit to their house after I was done helping Terry pull some weeds.

Despite the trouble I had finding a full-time job and my heightened cholesterol, my time back at Ridgewood during the fall was pretty good as I went out a lot with my friends and family. But that was the last bit of fun I had before the crisis occurred when 2020 started.

LIFE LESSONS

Present yourself more during an interview.

Always pay attention during a phone call.

Watch what you eat.

Stay fit.

Chapter 10:
2020, A. K. A. The Worst Year in the Whole World

Twenty-twenty, what a year! With the pandemic, deaths, small business shutdowns, protesting, rioting, delays with events and election campaigns, 2020 was a rough and challenging year for everyone in the world, my family and me included. I've read many people on the internet proclaim that 2020 was their worst year ever. I believe that there have been worse years, like the ones during World War I and II as well as during the Black Death and 9/11. Some people on the internet said they believed that 2016 was the worst year ever because actors like Carrie Fisher, Alan Rickman, Gene Wilder, and David Bowie passed away and Donald Trump became president, and boy, did that turn out to be a disaster. But I say that a lot of actors and famous people die every year. Sean Connery and Chadwick Boseman passed away in 2020, and that's just life. But Covid didn't just claim lives; it also destroyed our way of life, which took a long time for us to recover. My family's way of life was a victim to this travesty, too.

How the Bad Year Started

For me, the disaster started in March, the week after my sister's twenty-eighth birthday. Her party was in New York City. My family went to a bar with my sister's friends and cousin Charlie, who worked for a betting company within the industrial district of New York City, and we partied like crazy. I had my first drunk experience, as I drank so many beers during the party. Due to the loud noise and flashing lights, I couldn't tell what I was doing anymore. I was so hammered that I just couldn't stop talking, even when my parents were driving my sister's friend Nikki back to her house in Glenrock, New Jersey. Eliza's birthday party in New York City was the last time any of us were together, friends and family alike, before Covid hit and changed everything.

I had been focused on getting my internship as a graphic designer with NBC Sports, practicing my skills by making posters that were related to NBC. Within five days, the world shut down, and we had a new issue to navigate. I was on the verge of starting a new NBC training program in Stamford, Connecticut, in late March. I had already looked for an apartment and found one that would be perfect for a single guy in a small city. I was ready and excited for a new opportunity. Mom, Dad, and I were celebrating Eliza's birthday, and quietly I was celebrating the start of a new career opportunity.

One week after my sister's birthday party, I got home from a writers' workshop and my parents told me to watch the news of Trump's announcement that businesses would be shutting down to prevent the spread of Covid. After that, Dad told me that the NBC training program and Broad Futures Internship had been delayed from March until the fall. I was devastated by the news because I knew that the one chance I had to earn a full-time job had been taken from me.

Many of Eliza's friends lost their jobs because of the pandemic. Some of them had to move back to their parents' houses because they lived in the city and feared that they would get Covid. Eliza had to move back with us because of Covid. She began working at home, sitting in her room, often watching *Real Housewives* or *Vanderpump Rules* on her iPad. Dad also worked at home. He had a lot of calls with his coworkers on Zoom, and watched reruns of football, basketball, and baseball matches because they were delayed by Covid. Some of the basketball players got infected with Covid, and the planned March Madness of 2020 was canceled.

So, I spent the first week of the Covid shutdown hanging around my house while my dad and sister worked at home. Most of the time, I was writing *Party of Four Heroes* side stories; I was still feeling devastated with what was going on in the world after the shutdown. I did not like social distancing because I had become a pretty social guy after my college days were done. I wanted to be with people. My time alone reminded me of how some of the students at college I've mentioned were socially distant from me, too. But over time, I became used to social distancing. I was still sad by the fact that the pandemic screwed me out of the only close thing I had to a job.

I'd watch the news about current events every night from 6 PM to 7 PM with my dad and mom. I felt things weren't getting any better with the news reports of people dying and more businesses shutting down. At that point, my dad decided we should just move to Rhode Island for the month of April.

Our Retreat to Rhode Island

In Rhode Island, I learned how to shop on Amazon with my mom's account, and I got a PS4 copy of *Assassin's Creed Origins* that kept me entertained. Originally I was going to buy *Torchlight 2* for the PS4, but that got canceled by the gaming company. I also got a PS4 copy of *Trials of Mana* remake and played it during April.

During our month in Rhode Island, we were able to order from the restaurants in Jamestown, something the family and I didn't do in Ridgewood because Dad felt that we could get Covid-19 from takeout. We ordered from Winner Winner, which was a chicken place, and thought it was some of the best chicken ever because of how succulent it was.

Black Lives Matter

During the month of May, the pandemic was calming, and we went back to Ridgewood. But 2020 still had some other problems that started when George Floyd, an African American, was choked to death by a police officer for suspicion of scamming a store clerk with fake money. Everyone was outraged by how the cop killed George Floyd because of the color of his skin, which was an ongoing problem with the authority for the past sixty years. And so, some protesters created a campaign called Black Lives Matter. They had a series of protests in cities of the USA to demand that African Americans and other people of color not be treated badly by the police ever again. The news portrayed the Black Lives Matter events with scenes of people rioting in New York City, Boston, Washington, D.C., Minneapolis, Los Angeles, and Seattle. They broke into stores, assaulted people on the street, and burned everything on site.

To me, the protests and riots seemed partially sparked by the pent-up anger of people who'd spent the spring on lockdown because of the pandemic. Because of these events, my friends from the writers' workshop decided to join the Black Lives Matter rallies in Bergen County, but I focused on trying to avoid getting into danger. Part of me felt like I should have joined them and helped support Black Lives Matter while seeing how they were holding up during the lockdown. But I didn't know what to believe. I just wanted things to go back to the way they were before the pandemic. I did not like the "new normal."

Our Summer Retreat in 2020

I did have one funny story to tell about the summer of 2020. As my mom and I were figuring out how to rearrange my room, she asked me about multiplying, and I realized that I had kind of forgotten my times tables. For some reason, my mom laughed and yelled, "HELP ME!" Eliza came running into my room and tried to help her, but Mom said that I had forgotten my times tables. After we were packing up the tools needed to rearrange my room, I farted in my mom's face by accident. My mom, annoyed by my behavior, yelled again, "HELP ME!" She said she was going to jump off the balcony near my room because she blamed herself for raising an idiot like me for a son. But she also said she was joking and would never do that.

Another funny story to tell is that my sister had the entire family watch the Disney Plus movie, *Hamilton I*. She and I enjoyed the movie although my dad was making some funny jokes about the film. I joined in and made some funny riffs on the movie as well, which annoyed Eliza.

Summer Strengths Program

My parents had me sign up for the Summer Strengths workout program on Zoom, which was part of Broad Futures. I felt the idea was a waste of time because I was a Broad Futures alumnus. I'd already learned plenty from my 2019 internship. Being on Zoom wore me out every Monday through Friday, and I wanted to spend my summer swimming by the beach outside of our house and just do what most adults do, sip or chug beer, work on the internet, go out for walks, play catch, work out on my own, and read. But my parents told me that the Summer Strengths program would keep me busy for the first five weeks of summer.

I also saw Dr. Helper on a FaceTime call and talked with him about what I was up to during Covid and what he was up to as well. He was proud that I was keeping myself busy by writing and going outside for walks. I was relieved that he wasn't involved with the Black Lives Matter rioting in New York City. When he asked me about Floodo, I told him that he had passed away in 2019, and he was saddened by that news. Mom, who was with me during the call, later said it was odd he didn't know about Floodo. I also felt concerned that Dr. Helper's mind was beginning to slow down a bit as he was getting a lot older. I began to fear that Dr. Helper was going to die soon. I worried about whom I would turn to when I needed my medication filled out and whom I would talk to about what I'd learned or how to deal with my problems.

After I completed my Summer Strengths program, my dad suggested I help out around the house more so I would not lounge around all day reading comics and playing video games. I cleaned the windows, cleaned the showers and toilets, vacuumed the floor, and pulled the weeds. During that time, I decided to write what would become my first comedic fantasy series, *Fated Journey*.

How Fated Journey Came to Be

During the summer of 2020, I decided to write *Fated Journey 1* using the screenplay-writing format I had learned in college and write it as a kind of movie, comic, or video game with the references. This story is about a pair of eighteen-year-old twins named Samuel and Samantha, who have angel-like powers and team up with a womanizing prince, a princess knight, an emo ninja, an ogre barbarian, an annoying fairy brawler, a whiny gnome mage, an emo fighter, and a whiny priest to fight evil Romanesque empire before they resurrect a demonic god by traveling around a fantasy world. *Fated Journey* is a series with adult humor, sexual content, swearing, a lot of fourth-wall jokes, blood and gore, and a lot of the emotional baggage that many Japanese role-playing games (RPGs) have. I spent most of my afternoons writing. Back then, I called it *Fated Hero* but decided to change it to *Fated Journey* in order to avoid any possible copyright claims.

After I completed my script, I emailed it to my writers workshop and my family. My dad was impressed and said it should be made into a book, but he suggested I tone down the sexual content and swearing in order to gain a broader audience. The sexual content was the part where Samuel, the eighteen-year-old white-haired warrior, and Mikoto, the twenty-one-year-old emo ninja, had sex during the fireworks parade in her homeland. My dad said that if people, mainly parents, read those parts, they would think the book was smut and it might be deemed controversial and get banned.

I imagined that one of the parents would say, "Billy, what are you reading?"

Billy would respond, "Just reading *Fated Journey*, the best part."

And the parent would ask, "What part?" and then she'd grab the book from Billy and read the scene where Samuel and Mikoto made love. "Oh, my God, what kind of smut are you reading?" she would say.

My dad suggested that this book should be targeted toward young adults and tweens. But from my point of view, young adults and tweens are mostly interested in angsty teenagers who are moody for the sake of being moody. They identify with characters just like them in stories that take place either in a real-world high school setting or an unexplained post-apocalyptic setting. These are settings that have been done to death. Famous fictional creatures, like vampires, werewolves, zombies, and aliens are reduced to young adult heartthrobs, mainly male characters who just take off their shirts to turn on the female audience. There are love triangles that make the three characters, mainly two guys and a girl, look like jerks, which shows how sloppy the writing of the story is. Every single character is either decent, forgettable, idiotic, or unlikeable. And most of all, romance as the main focus of the story is either boring and uninteresting or problematic and abusive.

I believe that *Fated Journey* should be marketed toward a more teenage/college audience who enjoy a bit of toilet humor, swearing, blood and gore, sexual references, and humor targeted for a mature audience. I also want to target my book series to people who enjoy Japanese RPG as well as anime and Western RPGs and who enjoy likable or funny characters, well-written romances, and stories that are original and are not desperate cash grabs, a type of media that companies produce in order to gain a quick buck. I feel the comedy and parody of my novel should make the readers feel they are reading or watching one of those comedy movies with adult humor: *Happy Gilmore*, *Don't Mess with the Zohan*, *Stepbrothers*, *Ted*, *Pineapple Express*, *Hangover Trilogy*, *Anchorman*, *Dumb and Dumber*, and many others. And when I mention the Japanese RPG games and tropes, I'm including games such as *Tales of Berseria*, *Ni No Kuni 2*, *Final Fantasy 10*, *Final Fantasy 15*, and many others. The Western RPG tropes include Western RPG games such as *Dragon Age Origins*, *Dragon Age Inquisition*, and many others. Anime tropes include *Naruto*, *Attack on Titan*, *My Hero Academia*, and many others.

My Writing Process

Whenever there was a rainy day or snow day or cloudy day or sunny day, I would open my laptop at around noon or 1 P.M. I'd open a Word document and write one chapter for one of my *Fated Journey* installments. I would spend about three to five hours writing. Sometimes I would take a break to get a snack or something to drink. When I finished a chapter, I'd give my laptop a rest. Sometimes when it was running low on battery, I'd let it recharge. I would then reopen *Fated Journey* and go over what needed to be edited or what needed to be added. The hours were usually strenuous because I would stare at my laptop screen for a very long time. That's why I would take a snack break or go to the bathroom to stretch and let my eyes relax. But hey, at least I was doing something productive with my life. My fingers felt like they were moving fast as I typed and corrected words and sentences.

Working at Super Cellar

After our summer break, my mom saw a help wanted sign for a new employee at the Super Cellar Liquor store in Ridgewood. I decided to work for Super Cellar in order to do something during the fall. So I gave Joe and Brian, the owners of the liquor store, my resume, and did the interview with them. A few days later, while I was at Barnes and Noble, they called and said that I was hired to work for them.

I went to work for Super Cellar and was part of the stock crew. I would reorganize and stock shelves, take out the trash, help customers, and mop the floor. Because my work schedule took place from 4:00 to 9:30 P.M., I would have to eat dinner at around 3 P.M. and just eat snacks whenever I needed a break. But when my work schedule was altered from 3 to 9 P.M. during the holiday season, I decided to order pizza from the local pizza store, Santoni's, and ate it at a desk near the cheese shop.

The first time I ordered pizza from the Chow Now app, I requested a bottle of Pepsi. But when I got my pizza, I didn't realize how big the bottle of Pepsi would be, so I drank most of it and poured some of it near the trash bin because I knew that my dad wouldn't let me keep the big bottle of Pepsi in the house. A friend of my dad drank nothing but Pepsi, and he had a really bad kidney stone. Our family drinks seltzer water, orange juice, tea, milk, pomegranate juice, Sparkling Ice fruit-flavored water, and normal water at home, and we have beer and soda whenever we go out to a restaurant of our choosing.

The work was tiring, but I kept busy, walking around the store and checking to see if things were organized as they should be. That was also the first time I was able to receive paychecks from an app called When I Work, where I enter my work schedule stating what days I'm available. So I made myself available, and I have been working mostly Thursdays, Fridays, Saturdays, and Sundays ever since. I spent most of my weekdays during the fall of 2020 writing *Fated Journey* every afternoon. Sure, having to work on weekends could be a drag at times, but hey, just like my internship in Washington, D.C., there were no weekends and no summer breaks.

The Results

Later that fall, I had my blood taken. I toughened up because I have always been afraid of needles, and the last time I had my blood taken, which was in 2019, I chickened out and had to crush my mom's hand while the technician drew the blood. But this year I held myself together and got through it.

But when my mom had her blood taken at the same time I got my blood taken, she wasn't lucky because the needle accidently damaged her arm and didn't go to her veins, so she had to take another shot. I joked about it at mom's expense, and I realized that I was starting to turn out to be more like my dad, being a wise-cracker who makes jokes at other people's expense. I guess that's what happens when you spend too much time with family: you start to turn out more like them.

A few days after I had my blood taken, Dr. Rooney called to tell me that my cholesterol had lowered. My Cheerios and salad diet was working. My mom and I also learned we had both lost weight during Covid while many others had gained weight because they were trapped in their homes and did not get enough exercise. I think that moving to a summer home with some walking space and sunlight had paid off.

Moving to the Penthouse

There's a favorite place in the Ridgewood house, and that would be the third floor. Every night, I'd go up to the third floor and watch a marathon of *Family Guy*, *Simpsons*, and *South Park* episodes along with YouTube videos on my laptop. During the summer, I'd have to move down to the family room, where the internet is much slower, because the third floor gets so hot.

During the summer of 2020, my mom and I went to the local appliance store to find an air conditioner for the window on the third floor. The salesman was willing to recommend an air conditioner that his store sells, and like fools, we bought it. But when we got home and opened the box that contained the air conditioner, my mom and I realized that the air conditioner was too big to fit in the third-floor window. It was also incredibly heavy. So my mom and I decided to take it back to the appliance store and give it back to the manager, and he gave us a normal-sized air conditioner that was able to fit in the window of the third floor.

We had a Flood/Fritz family Zoom talk on, and I joked around about needing a place of my own to get a break from my parents. My mom would just "nag," and my dad would act like a "man-child." This resulted in my parents suggesting I live on the third floor until the Covid pandemic calmed down. Then I could find a place of my own to live in. I tried to apologize to my parents and explained that I was just joking, but they said that the third floor would be a great place for an apartment, so I moved there, and I have been on the third floor ever since.

When I moved to the third floor, I decided that it would be the best place to not only get some writing done, but also to do other stuff like solving puzzles and posting them on my Instagram account, reading books and comics, and lifting weights whenever I feel like it. My dad decided to call my new room the penthouse because the way the third floor was designed, it looks like an apartment with the bed, the closet, the couch, the TV, and the bathroom. But the shower in the bathroom is a bit too small for a giant like me, so I use the shower on the second floor.

Three Years Later

The curse of Covid upended the world, but we were lucky that no one in our family got sick. The negative part was that all our lives were put on hold for almost two years. Nothing was normal, and it was frustrating. Eliza's birthday was the reopening event for many friends and family. Mask rules were gone, and that was great news for me. It is much easier for me to read a person's emotions and feelings if I can see their entire face. With my learning differ-ence, it is challenging to understand people and their emotions. The mask world really made life more difficult. My parents always push me to look into people's eyes when I talk to them. I have a tendency to look around, in part because I'm uncomfortable staring directly at people, in part because there is always something to distract me. The face masks made the last two years that much more complicated and frustrating.

It's been two years since we celebrated Eliza's birthday in New York City in 2020. To me, it felt like the party was a little bit too loud. But in reality, the party was the last grasp of normalcy before the world shut down. Back then, I was excited to move to Stamford and have my own apartment. I had already looked for and found one that would be perfect for a single guy in a small city. I was ready and excited for a new opportunity. We were celebrating Eliza's birthday, but quietly I was celebrating the almost start of a new career opportunity.

I was so happy to see all of Eliza's friends enjoying the night and the party. The first few hours were awesome. But loud music and loud people can be overwhelming for me. I can only handle the chaos for so long. My world needs order, and the disorder of that party eventually made me uncomfortable. I had a few beers, and Dad says I was grooving to the music and kind of zoning out. It was a way to escape the chaos and control what I could control.

This world can be too loud, too big, and too crazy sometimes for someone with my issues. When I was three years old, I would pull Eliza's hair to get Mom's attention, and Eliza would say that I needed a cookie or orange juice or wanted to watch *Barney the Purple Dinosaur* on TV. I learned years ago that pulling Eliza's hair was not the solution to a problem. It was important that I found solutions to situations that could overwhelm my senses. Being at the party for two and a half hours was my limit... but there would be no hair pulling. I didn't think that would go over too well with Eliza's friends, and I certainly didn't want to be that guy to ruin her birthday. My solution was simple: leave the chaos and find some peace and quiet outside of the party, away from the honking car horns and swirl of people on the streets and sidewalk of the New York City Bowery. It was my escape, my way of taking control and finding my peace.

Plans for the Future

I don't know what's in my future yet. Maybe I could work with my Dad at NBC Sports in a communications or computer tech job. Or I'll be an author publishing more than just my autobiography. Some might say that I could be a script writer for TV shows, movies, or video games. Or I might have an office job doing basic office work. Someday, I would like to get my *Fated Journey* series published to the public.

Whatever the case, I'm just glad that I have a bright future ahead of me.

LIFE LESSONS

Sometimes things don't go according to plan.

Be careful of what you put in your stories.

Remember the audience you're trying to sell your book to.

Always have a work/writing process.

Find a way to get far from the crowd and noise.

— Chapter 11: —
A Life of my Own

I t was February of 2023, and I was still living with my parents back at Ridgewood. Even though the Covid pandemic had died down, I still needed a job and to move out of the house. I had less than eleven months to achieve my goal to be living on my own and becoming an independent adult by age thirty. This is when Broad Futures and Carolyn Jeppesen came back into my life. We had a Zoom call that would change my life forever. Carolyn said that there was an opportunity in the Logistics Department in NBC Sports, and that they could use a guy of my talents to help out the crew. It was a three-month internship to learn how to work in a big company like NBC.

I reported to Shannon Ward, who is one of the heads of the Logistics Department. On my first day, she explained what the Logistics Department does and my role on the team. The Logistics team handles any kind of delivery to NBC Sports from UPS, USPS, FedEx, and even Amazon. My first few assignments were mainly to make Excel spreadsheets of budgets and deliveries for golf and other shows. We logged everything into our system and then delivered to offices around the building that has almost seven hundred fifty people. Since the company was a year away from the 2024 Paris Olympics, I was also helping out the crew in an NBC warehouse in Monroe, Connecticut, every other Wednesday. Because I don't have a driver's license, I took the Metro Train to Bridgeport and an Uber up to Monroe.

Every week during the internship, I would have a Zoom call with Andrea, my mentor from Broad Futures, and we would discuss ways to improve myself at NBC Sports. She would give me a weekly goal sheet with a list of suggested improvements. While I'd learned a great deal from my previous two internships in Washington, D.C., there were some areas that need improving, such as repeating instructions to the supervisor in case I forget and to better understand them, always listening to people whenever someone is giving me instructions, ensuring that I completely understand the assignment before starting it, and being proactive about taking on new tasks if I have too much downtime.

Originally my internship was supposed to end in May, but since they liked me so much, Shannon offered me a job working for the NBC Logistics Department Mondays through Wednesdays. This was another big day in my life. I thought when my internship ended, I would have to go job hunting again, and that would be dreadful.

In Stamford, my team works in a place called Bay Area 10, which is where my Logistics coworkers, Tommy, Dickerson, and Andrew work. The four of us are interested in video games, movies, TV shows, and most of all, comics. We talk a lot during our free time about comic books and movies. We could have some sort of NBC podcast show where we discuss what's on our minds as well as our opinions on a lot of things. Not sure how we got here, but imagine a guy who didn't talk until he was five wanting to be on a podcast.

My Very First Apartment

My mom and I were looking at apartments in Stamford. We ended up at a building called the Urby. It is right near the Stamford Mall, so I can go to Barnes & Noble whenever I want and buy any book or manga. The apartment complex has its own pool, grill, workout center, and café, meaning I have all of these hangout spots to choose if I want to go out and socialize. The more I explored the various districts of Stamford, the more I ate at the city's restaurants, and the more I lived here, the more it became official that Stamford has become my new home now.

Chef Sam

Going out to eat all the time is not good for my bank account. I knew I needed to learn to cook for myself. When I first moved in, all I could cook was pasta, but as time passed, I felt that I wanted to cook more than just pasta and hot dogs. I asked my mom how to cook more meals for myself. She texted me recipes on how to perfect the meals she made.

The first meal I cooked in the apartment was steak. One interesting thing about the Urby apartment is that they have a set of grills within the garden section. Luckily, family friends, the Kincades, gave me a shipment of steaks of all kinds from the Peter Luger Steakhouse for my thirtieth birthday.

When I opened the package, I was surprised to see that the delivery also came with thick bacon, packs of ice, and some steak sauce. There were all kinds of steaks: ribeye, T-bone, Angus steak, and New York strip. It was hard for me to choose which steak I should cook first. My dad recommended the ribeye, seeing how it could be later saved for steak sandwiches for lunch.

Despite how freezing cold it was, I felt some sort of sense of joy in watching the flames jump up on the ribeye when I flipped it over in the night sky. It felt like I was living out one of those Burger King commercials that promoted their Whoppers, or like I was sitcom dad drinking a beer while grilling a big steak. When I added the finishing touches to my first ever ribeye, I took a picture of the steak I created and showed it to the Kincades as my way of thanking them for their generous gift. After I had my first steak that I cooked, it snowed the next day, and it was wonderful. It was like the whole city of Stamford was being blanketed in snow.

Even though I love steak, I know I can't eat it every day. The next meal I cooked was fried chicken. My mom suggested I'd use the Shake 'N Bake as she would use it for her chicken and pork chop recipes. She texted me a recipe on how I should make the chicken the right way. I made them in all kinds such as drumsticks, wings, and thighs, and pork chops.

The third dish I've learned to make is my favorite: lemon chicken. This was a challenge seeing how I usually use the oven to cook, but I have to use a frying pan in order to make the lemon chicken. But I'd had some luck using the frying pan to make my bacon during a weekend breakfast. After following the instructions my mom texted me, I spent a lot of time and energy on perfecting the way my mom cooked the lemon chicken. And after half an hour, I was able to make the lemon chicken that was close to my mother's recipe. Next up, I made a decent BBQ chicken.

There are a lot of other recipes I want to make on my own. Beef stew, scallops, a whole roast chicken, and most of all, spaghetti and meatballs. I'll just have to wait until fall comes around, and my mother will teach me the basics of cooking meals. I'll make the beef stew and spaghetti and meatballs during the weekends, since that takes a lot of time to cook.

Working for NBC Sports

Every morning I'm up at 7 AM. After breakfast, I walk a little more than a mile from my apartment to NBC Sports. In fact, I think I made the right call not to get a license. I have ADHD, so I would get easily distracted, and driving would be dangerous, which could result in a ticket for speeding or worse, getting in an accident. When I arrive at NBC Sports around 8 AM, I hang out in the commissary as I look at my phone for any kind of news update. Sometimes I chat with Jim if he's around. At around 8:30 AM, I walk to my cubicle and start up my computer so I can write down my daily schedule. Then at 9:00, I head to Bay Area 10 and prepare for a day of sorting and delivering packages.

My life at Bay Area 10 can be a bit fun, and I am often crazy busy with occasional lulls. I had to have a walkie-talkie with me at all times in case a delivery comes. There are about twenty-five or more boxes each day, mostly from Amazon, UPS, or FedEx, and I have to load them up on a cart and deliver them. Sometimes I feel like one of Santa's elves, but I love it.

Work in Monroe can be a lot busier than Stamford. I have to buy a Metro ticket the night before I head to Bridgeport. I get up early as usual and do the same morning routine. But I walk down to the Stamford Train station, which is a ten-minute walk from my apartment. I also bring lunch with me because the Monroe warehouse doesn't have a cafeteria. I spend most of my travels either listening to stuff on my phone or just gazing at the beauty of Connecticut. Once I arrive at Bridgeport, I take an Uber down to the warehouse. I begin work at around 1o AM by doing the same thing with my morning routine in Stamford. My role is to package a lot of stuff for the 2024 Paris Olympics. It is a lot of heavy lifting, strapping boxes, and loading them on skids to take to a wrapping machine. When I get back to my apartment on Wednesdays, I am really ready for a break.

On Thursdays, I get to work in the graphics department back in Stamford. It is great to be able to use my college degree in graphic design and learn how to build graphics for NBC Sports. In my graphics training role, I cut out headshots of football, basketball, and racecar drivers, using photoshop. I also do the same thing for logos of football and basketball teams and also work on golf. Graphic design is a bit challenging at times, as I have to be really careful in trying to make the image really perfect. But sometimes I would end up erasing some of the skin of a player or leave out some of the background.

One of my supervisors, Matt, noticed these mistakes and suggested I use a photoshop tool to fix the mistakes.

But I got stubborn and acted like I didn't need his help. Eventually, I thought about the lessons from Broad Futures, and Matt was just trying to help me, and I took his advice. I learned to use a colored background to find which parts of the background I didn't erase and just finish the job. That was one of the lessons I've learned on this job.

Working for NBC Sports may be a bit hard and stressful at times, but it is a job that helps pay for my rent and put food on my table. Most of all, I love being a productive member of the company.

Playing Pickleball

Even though I had made some friends at work, I had some trouble making new friends in the city. I went to bars and chatted with people, but I never really hung out with them more than one time.

When I had a Zoom call with Dr. Helper about making new friends in the city, he suggested that I go to church on Sundays in order to meet people. He also believed that this would be a great way to find a girlfriend. I wasn't so sure about that since a lot of people around my age don't usually go to church that often. So I wanted to find another place or activity to meet people.

My mom found out about a pickleball league in the Stamford Mall. She noticed that there were a lot of people around my age who have been signing up for pickleball, and it was becoming a success. Knowing that this is where people like me would go in order to make new friends, I decided that I should try pickleball.

During one cold weekend in January, I traveled to the pickleball court in the Stamford Mall and signed up for personal lessons with a pickleball instructor. She taught me the basics of how to play, which is a bit similar to tennis, but there's no hitting the ball with all of my strength. I was pretty strong whenever I hit the ball, causing me to screw up and shoot the ball right out of the court. Sometimes I would almost end up causing the ball to be shot into the ceiling or another court. I learned that pickleball is not about hitting the ball but about having fun. I also learned why this sport is called pickleball, as hitting it is just like getting the pickle into the kitchen. I always thought it would be funny and interesting to use an actual pickle to play pickleball as if I was using it as a tennis ball.

I've met a lot of people while playing pickleball. I've really bonded with a lot of them, especially Tommy, who was one of the instructors. He's actually a student at UConn, which is within the city itself. We all bonded and connected when he played a pickleball match and learned how to work together as a team.

Pickleball was the first step in my goal in not only making new friends and possibly finding a girlfriend, but also in being part of this city. Stamford is my new home, and I have to find a group or event to be a part of in order to know the city that I am a resident of. My other bets would include being involved in town parades, mayor election campaigns, Christmas Tree lightings, and so much more.

How Far I've Come in Life

I've come really far from when I was young. I've been through a lot of challenges in life, way more difficult than a lot of other people seeing how I have two learning disabilities, one that causes me to lose focus and the other that causes me to misinterpret what other people say. But I have a lot of people who are close to me, like my parents and Broad Futures.

Ever since I graduated college, all I wanted was to live in an apartment in a small city. Even though my parents let me use the third floor as some sort of penthouse, I felt that it wasn't enough for it to be an apartment. But thanks to both Broad Futures and especially my Dad, I have a job and an apartment. For the first time in my life, I was able to have a place to call home. I spent three years living with my parents when the Covid pandemic happened. I feared that I would spend my whole life living with my parents. But thanks to Broad Futures, I managed to get to not just an actual job but also an apartment of my own. I've managed to live on my own thanks to all of the skills my mother taught me such as laundry, cleaning, and cooking. Even though I just started cooking for myself, as I've expanded my recipes, it's only a matter of time before I can be as good of a cook as my mother.

I was afraid that if I failed at my internship, I would go back to living with my parents, probably for the rest of my life. But I managed to learn from criticism and worked hard in the internship. NBC Sports was impressed that they managed to keep me around since they needed some extra muscle for the Olympics. I also formed bonds with my fellow coworkers in Bay Area 10 and love sitting at lunch with tons of people my age. They made me feel like I was a part of a team, and I will do anything to prove that I'm worthy of being on their team.

When I was a three-year-old boy, some doctors told my parents that I'd never get into college or even attend school because I couldn't talk and was completely out of control. But now I'm thirty years old. I went to high school, graduated from college, and have a job at NBC Sports. For the first time in my life, I'm able to have a place to call home. It's all thanks to the life lessons I've learned over the years, especially the part where I've learned not to pull my sister's hair whenever I don't get my way. I wonder what other life lessons I'll learn for the rest of my life as time moves forward.

—Sam Flood

Acknowledgments

There are so many people in my life I want to thank for help-ing me not only write my life story but also get through the many challenges of my life.

I want to thank the teachers of Eagle Hill. Because of them, I was able to learn a lot of maturity, boundaries, and doing as I'm told.

The teachers of Craig High deserve a lot of praise and thanks. They helped me to move on from the worst year of my life at Maplebrook and got me on the right path to a college that helps people like me.

I want to thank every professor from Mitchell College. I learned so much from that college—how to take social cues, think-ing through what I should say, how to do a part-time job, working with graphics, and starting my path to the work environment.

Both Sarah Tuff and Tim Cary deserve the credit for help-ing me with my book. We would spend an hour every two weeks meeting about my writing and the edits they suggested I should take to improve my life story. They helped edit my autobiography by pointing out any error or plot hole as I wrote my book, and they gave me a lot of tips on how to improve my craft.

I want to thank my cousins, Hayley, Hugh, Charlie, Syd-ney, Allyson, John, Caroline, Briana and Clarissa. All through my childhood, my cousins were more than family; they were my friends who spent many holidays and summers with us. I enjoy the company of each cousin, and even if some of them are far away or have families and careers of their own to focus on, my family and I would often pay them a visit to see how they are doing.

I want to thank all of my aunts and uncles on both my mother and father's sides of the family. They have supported me and my family in their own way by spending a lot of time with us and helping each other out during tough times. I would like to send a special shoutout to Uncle Terry, who had me join his writers workshop, which was step one to creating this book. His love for fantasy and RPGs helped me become the author that I am now.

But the three people I want to thank the most are the members of my immediate family.

I want to thank my sister Eliza, for having the blondest and curliest hair any toddler would love to pull. Eliza is my best friend and the person I know always has my back. When we were younger and kids would tease me for being different, Eliza would always step up to protect me and stop the bullying. She also was incredibly understanding when I was whisked off to all the doctors' appointments and faraway schools—we were a team.

My dad has worked hard to provide for the family, the home we live in, and the chance for me to go to Eagle Hill, Craig High, and Mitchell College. He also inspired me to write my life story after he read all of my previous stories that I constructed with my imagination. He is more than my dad; he is also my friend, both at home and at work. It was thanks to him that I got not only a job at NBC Sports but also an apartment to live in.

Most of all, my mom deserves all of the praise in this world, especially from me. She has done so much for me since the day I was born. She has driven me to every doctor and every specialist to help me be the person I am now. She drove to every event of the schools I went to as a means of supporting me and Eagle Hill, Craig High and Mitchell College. My mom drove one hundred eighty miles every day to Eagle Hill when I was in sixth grade and seventh grade, from New Jersey to Connecticut. She had to argue with so many people who didn't believe in me or feel like I was nothing but trouble. She did all of this was because I was her son and any parent should never give up on their child.

About the Author

Samuel Elliot Flood, Jr. was born on January 1, 1994. He was supposed to be born December 16, but he waited two weeks inside of his mother just so he could be a New Year's baby. He likes to play golf, write, play video games, read fantasy novels as well as comics and manga, and watch anime and adult comedy. He was diagnosed with language processing disorder and ADHD, but those learning disabilities didn't stop Sam from graduating college. He majored in graphic design at Mitchell College and now works for NBC Sports.

A free ebook edition is available with the purchase of this book.

To claim your free ebook edition:

1. Visit MorganJamesBOGO.com
2. Sign your name CLEARLY in the space
3. Complete the form and submit a photo of the entire copyright page
4. You or your friend can download the ebook to your preferred device

Print & Digital Together Forever.

Snap a photo   Free ebook   Read anywhere

www.ingramcontent.com/pod-product-compliance
Lightning Source LLC
Chambersburg PA
CBHW020903310525
27535CB00021B/278